# Thursday Stories

Edited by

### Andrew Hiller
### Bryan M. Byrd
### Emily Wood

Montgomery
Writers

*Thursday Stories, Volume I,* is a collection of fiction stories and poetry. Names, characters, places, and incidents are the products of the authors' imagination. Any resemblance to actual events, locales, or persons, living or dead, is entirely coincidental.

Editors: Andrew Hiller, Bryan M. Byrd, & Emily Wood

ISBN        978-0-9969582-4-0
e-Book ISBN        978-0-9969582-5-7

First Edition

# Editor's Note and Dedication

The Northern Montgomery County Writers Group began long before there was such a thing as Montgomery County, Maryland. In fact, the group far predates the invention of the written word (which made early submissions particularly difficult.) Over the course of its history, authors have presented works in the fields of literary fiction, poetry, science fiction, young adult, picture books, graphic novels, memoir, poetry, and even real estate.

The group has evolved to serve three primary functions:

1) Support and critique: Members provide drafts of their work(s) at various degrees of completion. Mechanics, character, content, world building, story logic, etc. are all put under the microscope during constructive critique sections.

2) Networking: The Northern Montgomery Writers' Group members report to others about upcoming conferences, markets, contests, and publishing opportunities.

3) Performance: At least three times a year, members read from their works as invited guests at area libraries, bookshops, and other venues.

The form and shape of the Northern Montgomery County Writers' Group is ever evolving, but it owes a debt to its founders and leaders. So, this first volume of Thursday Stories must be dedicated to Jerri Reger and Linda Meyer. Their efforts at organizing, maintaining the temperature, and sustaining a nurturing environment for a bunch of creative knuckleheads deserves many Thursdays worth of thanks!

To learn more about or to contact the Northern Montgomery County Writer's Group go to-

https://www.meetup.com/The-Northern-Montgomery-County-Writers-Group/

# Contents

Thursday Stories

# A Book of Matches

## Andrew Hiller

Aged wood and heavy dust stirred. Eric Weiss placed a finger under his nose expecting his allergies to awaken and braced his left hand tentatively on one towering stack of books, but surprisingly, his nose didn't itch. For all the dust, age, and wear he could smell, no one in the bookshop sniffled. The shop owner lifted his spectacles to the top of his brow. The light that glinted off the glass made Eric squint.

"Ah," the shop owner smiled, "you're a reader. That's good. Well, let me see what you've got."

Creaking, the owner rose from his chair and took the resume Eric had hand-written and then rewritten three times before he was satisfied. The teen found it odd that there was no online application, not even a

downloadable PDF, but had dutifully filled out a form obtained, in-person, last week. When the owner lowered his spectacles to study the scant history on the paper's front and back side, Eric glanced away. Only one side of the man's white-whiskered face moved as if the other had been stilled by a stroke. A swirl of dust blanketed his left hand.

"You've never worked?" the owner said, blinking many times.

"Chores, sir." Eric answered, "I've been paid for chores." The old man sighed and collapsed onto a well-patched chair. He ruffled the few threads of hair he had left and placed the application on top of a silver-handled magnifying glass, then glanced at a stack and picked a book at random. He turned it over and replaced it. Eric noticed the fingerprints that rested on the old leather cover. Dust displaced.

"Why do want to work here?" The old man looked down at the neatly printed paper to find the boy's name. "Eric?"

Eric took a long slow look around the old shop. Towers of books teetered in haphazard order. The carpet remnants on the floor were stained and flecked with leaves from an autumn that ended months ago. A careful smile captured his face. Looking at all the dust and disorder, Eric thought what he thought when he first saw the help wanted sign. *This could be an easy job.* No dusting, no vacuuming, just piling books wherever you can find a space. *Yes, an easy job and some easy money.* He looked past the old man squinting intently at him. Eric Weiss shifted his own glasses and adjusted the tie he had borrowed from his father.

"I like books, sir."

The man leaned forward and motioned for Eric to come closer. He smelled of old wood pulp and leather. A calloused hand reached out to take Eric's wrist and pulled it until he pressed the applicant's fingers against Dumas' *Three Musketeers.*

"Can you tell," he asked, "if a book is crap?"

"What?" Eric said, then quickly added, "Yes, sir. I can tell if a book is bad."

"Just by looking at it?"

"You can't judge a book by its cover." Eric quoted.

"Bull," the shopkeeper said. He released Eric's hand and grabbed the Dumas. "You see the way the pages bunch up by the spine here?"

Eric nodded.

"Reader was in a hurry, wasn't he? Someone was breathing this book, tasting it, living it once, weren't they? Good book." He reached over and took a Bronte. "You mean to tell me you can't see the tears in this book? The twinning of the life of the book and its reader?" He paused, pursing his lips. "You're blind as a reader, Eric." He grabbed another, this time Twain. "You telling me

9

you can't see the laughter in here, boy? You don't understand books," the shopkeeper spat, "You only read pages. Words." Casually, he picked up another tome. "What do you see here?"

"I…" Eric stammered.

"That's right. There's nothing to see. This book was never embraced. It never kissed the life of a reader, didn't have the power to… or never found the right pair of eyes."

He put the book back.

"Stories have life, Eric. Good books have life." The owner sighed then as some customers turned at his raised voice. "You want to work here?" the shopkeeper asked again, "You've got to become a Yenta, a matchmaker. You've got to learn when the time is right and when it's not. Do you see?" The owner waved at piles upon piles of used books. "People change. Sometimes, their books no longer fit. Sometimes, they don't grasp what they need." He settled an Asimov in a stack of bodice-ripping romances. "Do you understand? Worst thing in the world is to let a good book go unloved."

The teenager smiled indulgently at the grown-up nonsense. His father warned him that everyone considered their job the most important job in the world. He surveyed the dust covered, disorganized mess that was the bookstore and then at the old man. It would be an easy job. He could deal with a little eccentricity. Eric Weiss nodded.

That was thirty years ago.

Eric's was the only standalone bookstore left in the city—perhaps in the whole state—that didn't sell espresso. A few of his customers understood. He called them patrons. These special few came to him and he led them to the books that were already theirs. The customers usually came in, wandered around, got confused, and left. Sometimes, they bought. Sometimes, they didn't. Usually, if they spoke to him at all it was to order him to find a specific book. A best seller. An award winner. A collectable. Some of them, the lucky ones, Eric thought, left with more than a book that simply won an award.

Eric Weiss thumbed through a crate of books a customer wanted to sell him and read each book's DNA. He analyzed the bubbles in the spine, the folds and arches in the pages. He probed for water spots and smiled when he found them. He thumbed the pages and let them roll by his ear, listening to the music of their pages. Four of the twenty books sang. They hummed with pages that turned unevenly and gave rhythm to his thumb's thrumming. He turned to the woman selling the crate and offered her twenty-five cents a book for the clean, well-preserved books. The woman frowned. He offered more for the damaged ones. When she asked why, he answered, "Because these books have lived. They will sell."

"But," she said, and then looked at the books he had chosen. Her eyes twinkled a bit. A part of her was relieved that the books he would pay more for were the ones she had treasured. Smiling, she took Eric's money. As she turned to leave, Eric stood and offered his hand. She paused and then shook it.

Eric frowned and with his left hand lowered his spectacles to the end of his nose. A stream of sunlit dust lay between them. He gripped her hand, pumped it, and turned it over. He bent slightly to read the hues of her skin and then looked into her eyes.

"I have something for you," the bookkeeper said.

"I don't have…"

"Don't leave, miss. This book is yours." He ruffled his hair in a way that resembled someone from his past. "Or at least, it should be."

"I really don't have the ti…"

He led her down aisles and through a maze. By an arch of books, he reached out and claimed one from the bottom. The thirty books above it barely moved. They just settled down. Still, the woman flinched as if she expected to be buried. He showed her the cover.

"I don't usually read…"

Eric's expression fell. He released her hand and his fingers caressed the book's cover. They traced a pocked path along the pages as if trying to show her something. She shook her head.

"I just don't like mysteries."

Eric Weiss touched her cheek and clenched the book solemnly in his hand. She edged backwards into a pile of books. They teetered and fell. The bookkeeper ignored the mess. His brow furrowed.

"You don't understand," he said, "This is your book. This book more than any other."

She began to retreat. Eric cursed himself for not having the manner of his mentor. He knew he shouldn't have touched her. "Wait," he called, fervently. She paused, but grabbed a heavy book in case she needed something to beat him away with. "Take it," he said, "Take it. If you like it, come back and pay for it." He removed his glasses and squinted at her with eyes painted from the colors of an illuminated manuscript. Eric stood very still and waited. She breathed, watching him. Slowly, she lowered the heavy hardcover. Old tinny jazz music, popular before each of their parent's birth, played overhead. The pair stared a beat longer, Eric rounded his shoulders and tried to look meek. Then slowly, she advanced, like a wild squirrel towards the hand of a child holding an acorn. Eric stood perfectly still. He could see her DNA, could see that of the book and how the two fit almost molecularly. That someone one hundred and twenty-three years ago had written this book for her… that this was her lover or at least one of the many love letters from the life within stories. It mattered.  The connection mattered. She snatched the book from his open palm almost like that squirrel and the spine tore nearly in two.

"I'm sorry," she said.

"Take it," he grinned, "take it. You can't injure what's in there."

She left. Eric sorted the crate as he was taught: books, collectables, and books of the heart. He sighed at the ravaged cover of a book that must have been reread hundreds of times.

"What makes them leave? Why do they think—" Eric sighed. The book wasn't dusty enough yet to truly speak to him. Still, he patted his latest orphan and placed it gently in a leather satchel to take home with him. It'd been a long time since he found a book that resonated with his own touch. A new book meant for him.

Eric Weiss startled at the sound of a bell. He looked up to see, *What was his name, Jamal? Yes, that's it.* Eric smiled welcome. A patron entered. He smiled and shook Eric's hand.

"Eric, this is my son. This is the first time he's ever been to a bookstore."

"I've been in a bookstore before, Dad." The son complained, but his father looked wistfully at the decaying brown, acid stained mounds, and said, "No, you haven't, son. This place is different. It's like... like... Santa's Workshop. Better! You don't..." the man stopped, perplexed, "...shop here."

His son looked perplexed too.

"Then why are we here?" And at that Eric and Dad both smiled.

"That," Eric answered, "Is what you will discover, I hope."

It took more than half an hour before Eric would allow Jamal to purchase a book for his son, but by the time the pair left they had found twelve. Father was pleased. The son wore a face of irritation, but he had already opened one book and found it hard to close. As the door closed, Jamal gave Eric a wink and flicked the bell. It tinkled like new wings.

Across from the store was an old city park, mostly benches and a few trees fenced in by an iron gate. Stepping quickly, Eric entered and settled on an old stump that had been sat on so many times that it almost seemed grooved and polished. The moon smiled and, in the background, car engines hummed a playful mantra. His eyes slowly surveyed the tiny brick façade of his shop, a shop that strained his father's love when he gave up college for it.  A shop that completed his life when the old man deeded it to him. He grimaced a bit, more out of habit than anything else, at the bold Starbuck's sign next to his faded hand-painted marquee. Truth was, had he not leased the property adjacent to the bookstore, he would have gone under many times. He wondered not for the first time if he had sold a bit of his soul. It hurt him every time a patron came into his shop carrying a venti.

15

"There is something wrong," he groused idly to a tree, "They pay fifty cents for a book that will enrich their lives forever and five dollars for a cup of coffee." The local squirrels offered no rebuttal. "With a book, you don't even need to ask if you get a refill." Shrugging, he opened his leather satchel and shifted his position such that the street lamp illuminated the pages to maximum effect. All these years later, it gladdened him that he still stumbled upon books meant only for him.

She came back. Very few didn't. With a most serious expression she placed fourteen dollars on the cash register. The shop dust seemed to shiver and retract from her money. Eric fingered the bills and frowned. Paper always told stories. They were the worst gossips. His eyes traced each crease of the crumpled bills lying before him. She gestured impatiently at the counter.

"Aren't you going to take it?"

There was something in her that needed him to be impressed that she returned and that she was one of the few honest ones left in the city. She looked crossly at him. Her hands kneaded the straps of a black pleather purse. The ends were thin and discolored.

"What's this?" Eric laughed, finally scooping up the ten and some singles.

"I wanted to pay retail," she said, stiffly. Eric stared at a chipped spot on the ceiling and began counting. He opened the register.

"Fourteen dollars for a book in that shape," he tsked, "I do an honest business." He handed back change. She left it on a scatter of paperbacks.

"It's…" She confided, "It must have been the best book ever written. How can it be out of print?"

Eric ruffled his hair and surveyed the thousands of abandoned children in his orphanage. He rose and took her hand. The muscles in her hand were tense, but her eyes rounded hopefully.

"People now-a-days," he whispered, "they have no taste."

She gripped his hand. Her nails pressed into his palm. He took a breath and was surprised to hear it shudder.

"I need…" she began, but stopped herself, "I… are there any other books here for me?"

He looked into her eyes and measured the space between her blinks, counted the rhythm of her breath and gauged the oils on her palm. Placing his spectacles down on a signed Steinbeck, he pressed a tissue to his nose. Something had changed. He could almost taste the alteration in her brain chemistry. The dust about her seemed to rotate back and forth warningly. His brow creased, as he measured the difference. He pulled his hand free from her grip.

"Well," she repeated hungrily, "Do you have anything for me?"

"No," Eric said.

"No?" she repeated.

"No," he answered.

She grabbed a book at random from the stack nearest him and shoved it before him.

"What about this one?"

"No."

She backed away and then lunged over the counter to grab both of his wrists.

"There must be something."

An explosion of dust motes burst into the air. They swirled away from the two like tourists fleeing bulls.

"I'm sorry."

"Look harder," she demanded, exposing the lines of her palm. Her smell was unknown to him, but it made his hairs stand to attention.

"I don't…" he began dismissively, "Palmistry is just… it was a lucky guess, miss. A book I once enjoyed that I wanted to share with someone."

A carnivore stared back at him and he trembled. With one hand, Eric pried loose her fingers. They both saw his blood at the same time. The woman gasped and let go.

She released him and fell onto a short stack of books. They scattered and she gave a surprised shriek. Eric ran around to help her off the ground. Dusting herself off proved nearly impossible. The impenetrable, nearly infinite dust of the shop imbedded itself into every inch of fabric on her body. Eric's eyes blazed, and without intending to, he stared. She turned to follow his gaze.

"You've found something?" she said, capturing his hands again, ignoring his wince when her fingers pressed once again on the area that her nails had pierced.

"No," he said, eyes still locked on that same corner of books. He tried to collect himself. His smile appeared false. "I'll pay for the dry cleaning, of course."

"Show me." She dragged him towards a shelf. Eric saw the book, studied the shelf, and then shook himself. He laughed self-deprecatingly. His fingers reached forward.

"It is nonfiction," he said with self-assurance, "but I am not sure it is quite…"

The woman took the book gingerly. Her fingers traced the title.

"Why is it two hundred dollars?"

"It is a collector's item. A semi-rare edition on military history by Hoffstern."

"Two hundred dollars?"

The dust marched to a Sousa beat. The cover flared off the light in her hands. Her oily skin smelled combustible. Eric swallowed, but walked over to the counter. The book was hers and it was not such a bad book. He had even thumbed through it himself once. Powerfully written, though he usually was not particularly interested in stratagem like *flanking* or *securing supply routes*. His stomach churned.

The woman looked uncertain now that the book had been named. She looked doubtfully at the title and suspiciously at him. She wandered away from the bookseller and worked her way back through the stacks where he had located her first book. Eric settled himself on his chair and waited.

"How come," she began accusingly, upon returning, "there are no two hundred-dollar books in that other section?"

"Miss," Eric reddened, "You need not buy that book. In fact, I prefer if you do not." But the book sang much louder for her than it ever had for him. She glared at her ruined clothes and then at him.

"What is your return policy?"

Eric blinked at her.

"No one has ever returned a book I have chosen for them." His ego bristled. "Read it then. Read it. If you do not like it, return it. I will be your private lending library, madam."

With white fists that finally twisted apart a purse strap, she pulled out her Visa card. Eric Weiss rang her up and watched her go. The door slammed shut. Leaning down, he picked up the book he was reading and bit his lip. *Why?* He wondered, *I have never before tried to refuse someone their book.*

The next book he found for her was Richard III. Eric happily handed her the play, relieved that it was the type of book that had many, many matches. She left equally happy as this was a used copy and not (as she half-expected) a first edition signed by Shakespeare himself. Still, the dust was as agitated as he'd ever seen it. Even worse than that one summer that Eric had offended it by trying out an air conditioner.

When she returned, Eric felt a sensation of déjà vu. Those round eyes, the pressed line of her mouth, a nose that breathed in rapid audible sniffs spoke of someone he had known from his past.

"That play," she began, "was precious. It was like… I guess I just never *got* Shakespeare before."

Eric smiled indulgently.

"All your books are so… won't you find me another?"

Eric stirred. *Precious?* Why did that word stick out? He studied her hungry, red-rimmed, rounded eyes again. *Precious*, he thought again and snickered. Perhaps she reminded him of Tolkien's little friend. She smiled back at him, but her lips retracted quickly, revealing bared teeth, and he felt her gaze intently. Eric's dust spoke portents, but the bookkeeper took a deep breath and forced himself to ignore the images.

"I think," he began cautiously, "I have a book for you."

She clapped her hands together, but then stopped suddenly and gripped the cash register, claw-like.

"Don't you need to study me?"

Eric laughed and bowed his head. He revealed to her a halo of honest baldness.

"My dear," he said, "It's not like that. I'm hardly a… soothsayer or wizard. As I tried to tell you before, I do not believe in palmistry or in tarot cards. There's no magic here. I've just been working in this shop for thirty years. And after thirty years, miss, you recognize patterns in your customers."

She tilted her head and turned to the stacks. The mismatched, leaning, unorganized towers stared at her. The book shelves lay cluttered not by author or category, but in some way that forced the wood to sag. His store was like a shaken bag of marbles. Eric held up his hands apologetically.

"It's a very complicated system, but there is a pattern," he answered her questioning shoulders. "You don't really believe in magic, do you?"

"No. No, of course not." Twiddling her new purse strings, she nearly snapped the pleather again. "So what book have you found for me?"

"Come, patron, I've been considering all week what I should offer you when you came back."

They worked their way to the back of the store. The bookseller climbed mountains of hastily tossed paperbacks as he followed the book's call. His eyes held a worried cast. *Would she be able to tell?* This would be his first lie, but perhaps… He pulled Hoff's *The Tao of Pooh* from the midst of an obscure pile where he had placed it earlier in the week. She snatched it from him. The dust seemed to wrestle and stagger against the acids on her fingertips. Eric breathed a quiet apology to the book. It was a very special book and undeserving of this miscast fostering. The woman carefully turned over the book in her hands. A frown creased her face. Disappointment laced her features at finding a book with Winnie the Pooh on the cover.

"It's hardly a children's book," he assured her. She glanced at it quickly and her Gollum eyes struggled to reconcile the offering with her needs. Finally, after minutes, her trembling hands relaxed and she turned towards the cash register.

Watching the poor book cry in its bag as it swung casually against her hip nearly broke Eric's heart. He faced the accusing dust and, for the first time in thirty years, sneezed. Dabbing his nose with a handkerchief, he sunk into his chair and failed to find concentration enough to read.

She came back around closing time.

"What is this?" She demanded, waving the book angrily in the air.

"I don't…"

"It's not the same."

Eric backed away, waving his hands in protest.

"Sometimes you must give a book time. It is a good book."

"It's not what I wanted." She practically growled.

Lowering his spectacles, Eric Weiss stood and gripped the ends of his counter. The bookseller said nothing. She glared at him. Still, he said nothing. Slowly, he placed his hand out. She looked at it and covered his hand with her own. Stiffly, he shook his hand free and pointed to the book. She opened her mouth. Wordless, his gesture made her retreat nonetheless. Again, he pointed to his open palm.

Gingerly, she placed the book in his hand. His hands closed over the ragged cover and he stroked the semi-glossed paper lovingly.

"Miss," Eric said finally. His voice rose quietly, a bare stirring of dust on the beach. "You are the first to ever bring a book back." He handed her a refund. "If… You are not welcome in my shop."

"What?" she said, her eyes rounding with need. "You can't."

"You have treated me with hostility, miss." His voice was cool. "You have even cut me. I have the right to turn away whom I wish."

"You can't." She repeated.

"Goodnight, miss. I wish you well." Slowly, Eric Weiss turned from her.

"Why," she pleaded, "Why did you lie to me?"

His shoulders hunched.

"That was the wrong book." She continued, "You and I both know it. It was not the book I wanted."

Eric Weiss turned around. His eyelids closed as he looked upwards.

"Because it is the book you needed. A book sometimes must do more than match your wants. A good book will sometimes help guide your actions. This book…" he cradled *The Tao of Pooh*, "is what you needed."

"But what about—?"

He cut her off abruptly.

"If I had given you that book, miss, it would have completed the plot, wouldn't it?"

She turned away from him. Her eyes lingered on the maze of books. A sandstorm of dust worked to bury the pyramids. Her fists clenched. She was not archaeologist enough to organize a dig. Finally, she looked back at him, but discovered something unrelenting in the set of his jaw. The bookkeeper would not change his mind. He would never choose another book for her again.

"What plot? What are you talking about?"

Eric Weiss bowed his head. A shaft of sunlight illuminated him… made him sparkle with faerie dust. Book dust. He measured his words carefully before answering.

"I hear that book call to you even now, miss, but you will never touch it."

"Why?"

"You would have killed him, your husband, yes?"

"You're crazy."

"Maybe. But am I wrong?"

Her Gollum eyes narrowed and a slick of sweat covered her suddenly. Her mouth opened before abruptly snapping shut. A grumble issued from her belly. One open hand crept forward, but Eric resolutely stuffed his own in his pockets.

"You don't und…"

She turned and left.

Eric sighed and apologized to the *Tao of Pooh*. He promised he would serve it better.

She never came back again.

*In addition to being a voracious reader in search of matches, Andrew Hiller is the author of* A Climbing Stock *and* A Halo of Mushrooms.

The Montgomery County Writers' Group encourages its authors not only to bring in their novels, short stories, and other works in progress. We also generate new works via exercises and prompts, as well as welcome work published elsewhere.

The following essay is not an exercise per se except that in some respects it is about exercise. It originated in a group blog stemming from William Jacobs' experiences as a way to share and describe physiological phenomena in an approachable, light-hearted manner that amuses while educating.

Hopefully, it will achieve that goal.

## Dyingman 21: Keeping Your Powder Dry (3/3/07)
### William Jacobs

Fellow blog denizen Beach Bum 6 wrote encouraging comments to me in a previous post. He is in better shape than I am and wished me luck in attaining similar health. He suggested that routine and regular exercise was of paramount importance and I'm inclined to agree.

The immune system's primary weapons are our white blood cells. These little beasties clean out dead tissue, germs, parasites, and debris by phagocytosis (eating the stuff.) They also incapacitate germs by producing proteins that match surface features of the germs much like a key fits a lock. The proteins are called "antibodies" which block the effective functioning of the germs so they find it difficult to prey on our cells. They also clearly mark the germs as foreign invaders to the phagocytes (white blood cells) that eat them.

The proteins that make up the antibodies are made of amino acids and the white blood cells get these from the food we eat. This can present a problem because we can't send a constant stream of amino acids to our white blood cells by eating all day. Worse, being sick often kills our appetites, cutting off that source of amino acids.

As a result, white blood cells get their amino acids from protein we've eaten before that has been stored in our muscles. Getting sick costs us muscle mass and the more muscle mass we have, the more building material we give our immune system to fight off the little buggers that make us miserable.

When gerontologists (doctors for the elderly) see a patient lose weight rapidly, there is cause for alarm.  Often older folks don't have much weight that they can afford to lose. The concern is that they are suffering from a serious infection.  Beach Bum 6 may be feeling as good as he is because he's got lots of ammunition stored up to fight off the bad guys. That feeling of well-being that physically fit people claim to have may be due in some part to the devastating effect their muscular bodies have on pathogens that try and fail to make them sick. They are just plain healthier and the old adage says that when you have your health, you have everything.

With this in mind, if I'm to stay a dying man for the nearly 30 years it will take to achieve Beach Bum's venerability, I'll need to take my fitness goals seriously. Not only does it suggest a method by which to cheat death for a longer time, but to enjoy that longevity.

I only wish it were going better than it is. I have sworn off the elevator in my building, but climbing stairs is starting to hurt my left knee. I have taken to climbing them one at a time with my left leg, two at a time with the right.

Will I be able to recover to the point where I can take two at a time with both or will my right knee decay from trying to pick up the slack?

Stay tuned.

## Will's Regimen:

Fitness Goals:
60 beats per minute resting pulse.
One mile jog in ten minutes or less.
100 lbs. -15 times - two cycles.

Current Fitness Record:
Pulse: 60 beats per minute (unconfirmed)
Mile:  4 minutes jogging.
Weights: 5 days of 75 lbs. x 2 complete cycles 3 sets of 90 lb. bench presses.

RECENT SYMPTOMS : weak, painful knee. (left patella).

ONGOING SYMPTOMS:  Inflexible pinkie and middle finger of right hand. (65 and 85% flexibility, respectively); Pain between 1st and 2nd toes of right foot.

DIAGNOSIS: Recovering stress fracture of secondary phalange of right hand.  Possible joint damage in knee. Hyperextended tendon in foot.

ONGOING TREATMENT:  Exercise, gentle stretching of fingers, increase consumption of leafy greens.

PROGNOSIS FOR FOLLOWING WEEK: Tiny increase of flexibility of fingers.  Improvement of right foot.  Gradually strengthening knee.  General good health.

The End
Linda Meyer

"Julia? Julia, are you awake?"

I opened one eye and peeked out; Dad was standing at the end of my bed in the 'Super Dad' T-shirt we had given him for Father's Day. He held two bagels and a huge coffee cup that read "Climbers Reach New Heights."

"Morning, Super Dad!" I smiled at him as I stretched.

"Good morning, Super Julia! Do you want to help pack the car for our camping trip?"

Nodding, I threw back my covers and jumped out of bed, catching a glimpse of myself in the mirror. My short brown hair was sticking out on one side; the shorts and T-shirt I had slept in were wrinkled. Green eyes, like my Dad's, stared back at me. I patted my hair down, straightened my shirt and slipped into my shoes.

"Here," he said, tossing me a bagel, "so you have the strength to load the car!" We both laughed and headed toward the garage, munching. As we passed through the kitchen, my mother waved to us from behind the fridge door. I heard the clatter of ice as it fell into the cooler. In the garage, sleeping bags, tents and chairs were already stacked up.

"Okay," Dad said, rubbing his hands together as he surveyed the pile of camping gear. "First, let's get the tent and chairs in the van."

Making a few trips to the van before realizing I was working alone, I turned around to see Dad standing over his climbing equipment. He opened the lid of the box, dug around in it for a minute before picking it up and bringing it to the van.

"Move those chairs over for me, will ya?" he grunted, as he carried the trunk. I pushed aside the chairs. The heavy trunk made a clanging sound as it landed.

Mom came into the garage, squeezing my shoulder as she passed by, before giving Dad a quick hug. "Cooler's ready, Jim."

"Great! Let's get those lazy sisters up so we can get out of here."

Turning to me, Mom said, "Julia, will you please go and wake your sisters? Bagels and juice are on the table."

"Sure, Mom." I went to Anna's room first; she was asleep on her stomach, with her butt in the air. She was wearing a pink princess dress that had seen better days. The pink, silky dress was up around her knees, and layers of ripped netting gave way to flowered underwear. Her blond, wispy hair splayed out wildly on the pillow, obscuring her face.

Anna, time to get up." I gently shook her. "We're going camping today!"

"Today?" Anna sat up, her blue eyes staring at me. She wiped the hair off her face and gave me a big toothless grin as she rubbed at a big grape juice stain on the front of her dress.

"Yes, today; now, come on. Where are your shoes? Go potty and I will get you a bagel and some juice."

"Okay." She slipped off the bed before slithering, snake-like, underneath it.

"What are you doing?" I asked, poking my head under the bed.

"Getting my stuffies for the trip."

"Get your shoes and come on! I have to wake Kristy!"

My big sister's room smelled faintly of smoke and strongly of air freshener. Even the window, left open all night, failed to remove the smell. As for Kristy, she was on her back, her arm over her forehead as if blocking a blow. Nice try, I smirked, as I stood over her.

"Get up!" I yelled.

Kristy sat up, her arm flung wide and hit me in the stomach: "What the hell, Julia! What time is it?"

"Camping time!"

She put her feet on the floor and glared at me. "I hate you."

"Whatever, you're lucky I woke you, and not Mom! I can still smell the cigarettes." I rubbed my stomach, still smarting from her blow. "I won't tell if you get up and get going; I really want to go camping! We never do anything fun. Let's go!"

Kristy fell back onto the bed. "I hate bugs, I hate the outdoors, and I really don't understand the whole rock climbing thing. I want to stay home and go to Andrea's party."

"Yeah, well, boo hoo for you . . . Let's go, Smokey." Kristy's pillow hit me on the side of the head as I tried to escape her wrath.

"Are they up?" Mom asked, as she passed me in the hall, carrying more stuff.

"Yep, I'm getting their breakfast right now."

I heard the bathroom door shut and saw Anna still half under her bed as I brought her bagel to her. I pulled her out by her feet. Dust bunnies were stuck in her hair and her arms were full of dusty stuffed animals.

"Anna, the van is full. I need somewhere to sit, too! You can't bring all that stuff."

"Don't worry, silly. We can all hold some, except Daddy, he's driving," Anna said, then yelled, "I need a bag!" as she ran down the hall, returning with a big plastic shopping bag. After loading it with stuffed animals, Anna dragged it down the hall to the kitchen. I followed, still carrying her bagel.

Kristy came into the kitchen wearing makeup, short shorts, and a halter top that barely kept her little boobs in.

I laughed; "You look ready for camping!"

"Shut up, Julia," she said, as she poured a glass of juice before going back down the hall. She returned with her back pack slung over one shoulder.

"Mom said to grab a bagel."

"Great, my last meal is a stupid bagel," she snapped.

"I hope so!" I mumbled, as Kristy aggressively bit off a piece of bagel, chewing loudly.

Mom came into the kitchen and poured herself a cup of coffee before turning to look at us. Her cup was halfway up to her mouth when she saw Kristy. Her eyes went wide, coffee spilling onto her T-shirt.

"Kristy! Go change right now! You are not wearing that. Go put on a different T-shirt, and shorts that actually cover your butt!"

Kristy looked down at her shirt, pulled it down and looked mom straight in the eye. "What's wrong with this outfit?"

Mom took a step toward Kristy, "Seriously? I'm not doing this right now; go change."

"Fine!" Kristy brushed past me again, pushing me into the wall with her hip as she passed.

"Hey, Mom told you to change, not me; I think it's the perfect outfit for camping!"

I herded Anna and her bag of stuffed animals out to the van and got in, but Anna dawdled behind the van while Kristy entered, wearing an old T-shirt and gym shorts. She ate her bagel and slurped her juice loudly. "What is taking so long?" Kristy complained, "Come on, let's go!"

Kristy leaned between the front seats and honked the horn using her bagel for leverage. Dad was sitting in the driver's seat drumming his fingers on the steering wheel to a beat only he could hear. I looked out the window; Mom and Anna were playing tug of war over the bag of stuffed animals.

"Anna, you can't bring all this stuff with you!"

"But, I need them, Mommy!"

"We are only going away for two nights; you can leave some at home!"

"I did, Mommy, I left Roger, Steve and Ed."

Anna seemed to be gaining strength as she pulled; Mom's will seemed to be weakening. Anna's head bobbed up and down as she pulled and her sturdy little legs held their ground, her princess dress swirling around her feet as she tugged.

"Dad," I touched his shoulder and pointed at the back of the van, "Mom needs you."

"Oh, right," he laughed. Jumping out of the car, he took the bag from both Mom and Anna and put it into the back of the van between all the camping gear. My parents got in, Mom slammed her door.

"Pick your battles, Kay, that's what you always tell me. I didn't think you were going to win that round, she looked like she was up for a fight."

Anna wormed her way between us, squeezing some of her stuffed animals onto the seat.

"Anna, we have to sit somewhere, too. Dad, why can't I sit in the back? Anna and her crap are taking up the whole seat," Kristy whined.

"Sorry Kristy, the five of us have a lot of stuff, the van is full. You guys are just going to have to figure it out. It's not that far."

"You're fine, Kristy" Anna said, petting my sister's arm.

"Whatever," Kristy grumbled. "Dad, how long of a ride is it?"

"It's about an hour and a half; settle in, we'll be there before you know it. Anyone want to sing a song?"

"I do," Anna's head bobbed up and down.

"Okay, how about 100 bottles of beer on the wall?"

"No, Daddy, I don't like beer, how about we sing about juice?"

Dad laughed. "Let's sing Row, Row, Row Your Boat, instead."

She and Dad sang a few rounds before Anna turned back to her stuffed animals.

Anna hummed and played with her stuffies the whole way. I squished myself up against the window, watching the scenery whiz by while Kristy read her favorite book, "Go Ask Alice." My parents talked quietly in the front seat. The sounds of their voices lulled me, and the time passed quickly.

*     *     *

As we pulled into the park, I craned my neck to look up at the giant bowl-like wall of rock surrounding the lake. Trees sprouted from the tops of the rock and were mirrored in the water below, making it look like a forest was under the water. Climbers were swarming the rocks; ropes crisscrossed the biggest cliff wall like a web. Dad parked near the Rangers office and went to get us a camping spot.

The sound of splashing and laughter greeted me when I opened the van door. Anna's stuffies spilled out onto the parking lot.

Anna screamed, "Get them before they run away!"

"Huh?" I stared as Anna flung herself out of the van and started to scoop up her animal.

"Stay, stay, stay," she demanded of them; they did.

I laughed, "Where do you think they're going?"

"Back to the forest, you dummy, to be free, but they won't be safe there; they need special care."

"You need special care," I mumbled under my breath, as I made the crazy sign with my finger.

Kristy hopped out of the van. "Wow, those cliffs are really big!" she shaded her eyes and stared up.

"Some are, some aren't," Dad replied, as he walked back to the car, placing the registration on the dashboard. "We'll get a better look at them later when we take our hike."

"What hike?" Kristy asked. "You never said anything about a hike! I want to go to the beach and lay out in the sun!" She pulled out her lip gloss and re-applied.

"You'll get plenty of sun setting up camp and hiking," Dad said. "Okay ladies; let's get a move on to the camp site. Back in the car everyone."

"Can't I walk?" I asked, watching Anna carefully line up her animals across the seat.

"No it's a little too far; it's just a few minutes more."

I perched on the edge of the seat, not having the energy to argue with Anna. My seat belt slapped against my leg.

*　　*　　*

The campground in front of me unfolded, like a little city. Cars were pulled into campsites, tents and trailers were neatly sitting next to picnic tables and fire rings. People were clustered around their fires. Towels and clothes hung from clothes lines strung between trees, smoke from the camp fires billowed high above the tents and trailers. The smell of roasted hot dogs seeped into the van.

We stopped to let some kids cross the road, and then again to wait for a group of boys, playing catch, to move out of the road. Dogs barked, babies cried, birds sang; it was a symphony of sounds.

When the van stopped for the last time, we all piled out. Dad opened the back and started unloading the tent, chairs and a small grill. I carried the chairs over to the fire and set them up while Kristy and Anna headed into the woods for firewood. My parents worked on setting up the tent, poles clanking as they hit the ground and canvas billowing out before it settled flat, waiting to become our home.

After the tent was set up, Mom started making lunch while Dad went into the woods to gather firewood. I heard him singing one of Anna's favorite songs, a silly song about watermelons. He returned dragging a huge tree branch. Kristy and Anna followed behind him, dumping their small collection of sticks on the ground. Dad quickly chopped the tree branch into pieces with his axe.

Soon, Mom called us for lunch. Sitting at the scratchy picnic table, I tried to listen to Dad talk about our hike, while Anna hummed next to me and played with her food. Her little legs swung back and forth on the bench. Every so often, one leg would swing wide and kick me in the calf. Dad studied a hiking map while we ate.

"Ok, so after we eat, we are going to hike up to the top of the cliffs that I will climb tomorrow. This brochure says there's an easy trail up to the top, we can do easy. Can't we girls?"

Four heads nodded; Kristy looked less than thrilled, Anna didn't know what she was saying yes to, and Mom and I were all in.

"Then," he continued, "after we finish the 10 mile hike—"

"Ten miles?" Kristy yelled, "Dad!" She stood up.

"The hike is only a few miles, Kristy, I was just kidding. Sit down and finish your lunch." He tried to take her hand, but she pulled away, pouting while she ate the last of her cookies. "As I was saying," Dad paused and winked at Kristy, "after the hike we will go swimming before dinner."

"Swimming?" Anna stood up on the picnic bench, her little body swaying. "I love to swim! Daddy, will you throw me up in the air?"

"Yes, Anna, I will throw you high in the air!" Anna giggled.

After lunch, Dad marched us out of the campsite, and down the road. He stopped once to check the map, before continuing onto a path in the woods. "We are looking for the Blue Diamond path," he announced, as he moved quickly down the dirt path.

"Jim, you are going to have to slow down!" my mother yelled, as she ran toward us, Anna dangling from her hip. Mom's shirt had ridden up and I could see her belly hanging over her shorts. She shifted Anna up higher on her hip and pulled her shirt down, hiding what she called her baby fat (She said she called it that because it was that fat she got from having three babies.) Her short brown hair was already plastered to her forehead, one lock covering her right eye. She brushed it out of her face with her forearm. "Anna can't move that fast," Mom panted, as she lowered Anna to the ground.

"Oh, right," Dad replied, before swinging Anna high in the air onto his shoulders, pushing the puffy princess dress out of his face. "Want a ride, Anna?"

"Yeah!" Anna clapped her hands and grabbed onto Dad's forehead.

"Anna, sweet heart, you can't cover my eyes with your hands or I can't see."

"Sorry, Daddy!"

We marched in a line, Mom taking up the rear, like ducks in a row. Soon, we were climbing up. Dad found each of us a hiking stick.

"I want a stick, Daddy," Anna demanded, patting Dad on the head.

"Anna, you can have a walking stick, if you're going to walk. Are you going to walk?"

"No Daddy, I like it up here, but I still want a stick."

Dad sighed and started to bend down to get one, until he saw my mother shake her head. Even I could picture what would happen if Anna had a stick; Dad would take the brunt of that.

"Anna, how about a flower for your hair, instead?" Mom asked, as she pulled a cluster of wildflowers and handed them to her.

Anna smiled and nodded, taking the flowers and setting them on top of her head. "Thanks Mommy; I'm a princess!"

I laughed, watching the flowers bob along, high up in the air, riding the waves on her blond wispy hair.

"How much farther? Kristy asked, stopping to lean on her stick for the thousandth time.

"Far, if you don't keep moving!" I snapped at her; "You can't keep stopping!" I leaned over to whisper,

"Come on, Smokey. You can do it!" She swatted at me, but missed.

"Bitch!" Kristy mumbled under her breath.

"Mommy, I have to go potty," Anna announced, from up in the clouds.

"Great," Mom rolled her eyes, as Dad swung Anna down to the ground.

"Okay, Anna, but there is no potty here, you are going to have to go in the woods." Mom took Anna's hand.

Anna's eyes got big and round, "How?"

"I'll show you, come on." The two disappeared behind a tree, but their voices carried out to us.

"Pee on the ground, mommy? Yuk!"

"Anna, either you have to go or you don't."

"I do."

"Then this is how you have to do it."

Dad pulled a jug of water out of his back pack and filled some cups with water. I took a deep drink and sat down on a log. Kristy plopped beside me, rolling the log back. I lost my balance and fell back into the brush, spilling water on my shirt.

Kristy glanced back, "Sorry."

"Sure you are!" I struggled to get back up on the log as Mom and Anna popped out of the woods.

"We're done," she announced, as she wiped Anna's hands and legs with a wipe. "No water for Anna, I don't want to have to do that again!"

Dad swung Anna back up onto his shoulders, causing her flowers to flutter to the ground, leaving a trail as we walked.

My legs ached when we finally reached the top. Around us, people were sitting on top of the cliffs, some with ropes attached to them, others just enjoying the view. I walked to the edge and peered over; it looked like a sheer drop all the way down into the lake. Even repelling with ropes, it would be scary; I couldn't imagine how anyone could get up or down the wall of rock without ropes. Staring down, I saw waves splash against the rocks, swimmers scattered across the beach, and boats dotting the lake. My heart skipped a beat as I turned back to Dad.

"Dad, it looks really steep! How do you get down that?" I asked, peering over the edge.

He nodded with excitement, not hearing my fear. "Well, for this climb, I think I'll free climb, I do it all the time on rocks just like these." He flexed his muscles, making his shirt sleeves dance. Anna laughed, and I looked over the edge again. "Nothing to worry about ladies, it's a piece of cake."

Kristy and I looked at each other before looking down the sheer cliff to the water one more time. Mom held Anna's hand as they stood well back from the edge. Anna was pulling toward us, but Mom held her back.

"Mommy, I want to see the water," Anna whined.

"We are going to stand right here Anna, little girls can't get too close or they might get hurt." Mom looked at Dad intently as she spoke; he looked away.

"Okay, who's ready to get back to camp so we can go swimming?" Dad asked, as he turned away from the cliff.

Three hands went up. On the way back to camp, we took turns peeing in the woods, ate a snack and suffered through a sit down strike from Kristy. We staggered into the campsite and collapsed into the chairs as Dad piled wood in the fire ring so we could later make quick work of starting a fire.

"Who wants to go swimming?" Dad asked.

"Not me, I'm going to take a nap," Kristy moaned, as she unzipped the tent and collapsed onto her sleeping bag.

"I'll go." I got up slowly from the chair, stretching my sore muscles.

"Me, me, me, me," yelled Anna, running into the tent. "I'll get my suit on."

"Julia, can you please help her?"

"Sure, Dad, we'll be right out." I helped Anna into her suit. Kristy smirked at me as I tried to change without letting her eyes bore into my chubby flesh. I changed quickly, kicking her in the foot on my way out.

"Weirdo!" I bellowed, as Anna and I zipped the tent back up and joined Dad at the van.

At the lake, people were packing up for the day, the sun was beginning to set over the cliffs, and the sand was cool on our feet.

"Perfect," Dad said, as he set down our towels. "Everyone is clearing out, just for us!" He laughed.

"Throw me, Daddy, throw me!"

"You have to get in the water first!"

I stuck my feet in and felt the cool water lap at my skin. The further I went, the cooler the water became; before long, I was up to my chest. I dove under, opening my eyes in the murky water, seeing only a greenish glow from the setting sun. I felt something rub against my legs as I swam into deeper water. I turned when I heard Anna yell and watched as she flew in the air, into the water. Dad caught her as she went in, before she went under.

"Again!" Anna yelled. I floated on my back and studied the cliffs; they were still teeming with climbers. We splashed and played until the sun dipped behind the cliffs.

"Julia, we should probably go back; Mom should have dinner ready by now."

"Okay." I swam toward the shore as Dad dragged Anna out of the water.

"No, Daddy, not yet!" She yawned widely, her pruney toes burrowing into the sand.

"Anna it's time for dinner. Mommy is cooking your favorite meal. Aren't you hungry for hot dogs? We can't miss that, can we?"

"Hot dogs and chips?" Anna asked.

"Yes, hot dogs and chips." Anna stood up, took Dad's hand as we moved toward the van.

At dinner, Anna's head rested on the table as Mom worked to get her to eat a few bites before falling asleep. She rallied for S'mores, but was tired by the time we started our last trip to the bathroom for the night. Kristy, Anna, and I took a flashlight and made our way down the path to the bathroom. Kristy led the way, lighting up the path. Anna was in the middle and I followed, the dark swallowing me up. I sped up, chasing the light.

The bathroom glowed in the darkness, light spilling from the high windows. The door squeaked loudly every time someone came and went. Inside, the brightness made me blink, after the darkness of the woods. Overhead, the lights attracted millions of bugs, who quickly sizzled on the hot surface. Dead bugs dotted the counter and floor. We brushed our teeth, went to the bathroom, then headed back to the campsite.

On the path back, Kristy stopped; "Is this the right way?" she asked, sweeping the flashlight back and forth into the woods.

"Think so," I answered, turning to look around. All the campsites looked the same. Fires illuminated faces, voices danced in the breeze. We walked further until we hit a road.

"Uh oh!" Kristy cried out. "We didn't cross a road on our way here!"

Anna started to cry.

"Anna, stop!" I took the flashlight from Kristy. "Let's just go back and see if anything looks familiar."

We turned back and stood at the bathroom door pointing the flashlight down all the different paths. Anna sat down in the dirt and rubbed her eyes. Kristy tried several paths, coming back each time shaking her head.

Baffled, we sat down. People came and went, the door squeaked, toilets flushed and flashlights danced in the woods between campsites and the bathroom.

"Kristy, Anna, Julia!" Dad's voice called us from the other side of the building.

"Dad, we're over here!" I smiled as Dad rounded the corner; relief swept through my limbs and heart.

"Girls, where have you been? We were getting worried about you!" Anna flung herself at him, clinging to his legs. He reached down and picked her up.

"We got lost," Kristy told him, "We tried several of the paths, but none of them was right, so we just sat here to wait."

"That was the right thing to do," Dad nodded, "Good job, girls. Now, let's get back to camp, it's getting late."

Staggering into the tent, I settled myself between my sisters, my position in life, and listened to the lull of conversations around the dying fire, the hoot of a nearby owl and the soft snickering of my sister's snoring. I woke several times that night, once when "Hoppy" whacked me in the face, and again when Dad's snoring got loud enough to scare off all the bears for miles around. I eventually found comfort in the familiar sounds of my life and dozed off.

I woke up to the sound of my parents talking quietly the next morning. I rolled over, closer to the window to listen, pulling one of Anna's stuffies out from under me. I threw off the covers and crawled to the tent window closest to my parents. Mom's voice rose a bit and I strained to listen to what was being said, but I couldn't hear their conversation.

Crawling to the door, I unzipped the tent and joined my parents outside. The campground was waking up, the smells of coffee and bacon were in the air, voices could be heard through the trees.

"Morning, Julia," Dad greeted me, as he sorted through his climbing equipment.

"Dad, aren't you taking the ropes?" I pointed at his pile of stuff. "The cliff you showed us yesterday was really high."

I grabbed the ropes, dragging them over to where he was standing. They were heavy, the clips slicing a zigzag snake into the dirt. Mom watched us, silent, frowning, lips pressed together.

"Don't need 'em for this climb," he laughed, patting my head. "Don't worry Julieboolie; I'm just climbing down to the water. It's a short one this time. I'll be done in time to have a picnic and a swim, as long as Mom doesn't forget to pick me up in the boat."

He smiled again. I frowned, my brows furrowed, Dad looked at me,

"Look, I wore this bright neon yellow shirt so you will be sure to see me." Last night's hot dogs and S'mores rolled in my stomach.

Waving, he walked away from our campsite and tripped over the ropes. He laughed, pointing; "See, I don't need the ropes, they tried to kill me!"

Mom pursed her lips, "Julia, please go get your sisters up, so we can get out on the lake before he's done with his climb."

I rolled my eyes. Why couldn't Mom wake them up? Why did I always have to be the one to argue with Anna and Kristy? I knew for sure Kristy was going to give me a hard time.

Maybe that's why.

When I peered into the tent and saw Anna on her back with Hoppy clutched in one hand, thumb in her mouth, I decided it was time for a little payback. I crept around to the back of the tent and scratched lightly against the canvas. Peeking in the window, I saw they were still asleep, so I cupped my hands around my mouth and growled like a bear.

"Kristy, do you hear that?" I heard Anna's little voice ask.

"Hear what? Anna, go back to sleep, stop bugging me!"

"No, Kristy, I hear a bear!"

I roared again.

"Go, Anna, go! Get out! Go find mom!" Kristy yelled. Stealing another look, I watched the chaos. Both girls flopped around, getting tangled in their bedding, tripping over each other, trying to escape the tent. I burst out laughing.

"Julia! That's not funny!" Kristy yelled, red faced, as she came around the tent, and shoved me to the ground.

"Hey, cut it out! I was only joking around!"

"You scared Anna half to death."

"I scared you, too!" I laughed. "And by the way, run from the bear, not toward it! And remember you only have to outrun Anna; she'd make a nice little bear snack!"

"Girls," Mom called from the picnic table, as she filled cereal bowls and poured milk. "Come on, let's get going." Anna came to the table, glaring at me as she ate.

"You're mean," she mumbled as she chewed loudly, bits of cereal stuck to her chin.

"Scaredy cat; there are no bears out here!"

"How am I supposed to know that?"

"Well, Kristy should have known." I laughed again as Kristy flicked cereal at me.

Finally, we were dressed and packed up. Just as we were about to leave the campground, Anna came out of the tent dragging her huge bag of stuffies.

"Anna, are we seriously going to have this conversation again?" My mother sighed . . . "You can bring whatever toys you can carry."

Anna filled a bag with toys and dragged it behind her.

"How are you going to get that all the way to the lake?" I asked her, as she pulled the bag, bumping it over roots and rocks.

"I just will," she told me.

"Fine, but if you don't hurry, we're going to miss seeing Dad!"

Anna picked up her pace, "Coming," she wheezed, as she dragged the bag. She didn't get very far before her cheeks started turning red.

"Give it," Kristy demanded, taking *Stuffy's Ark* from her. Anna took two animals out of the bag before releasing the handle.

"I don't know why you spoil her; you should have just left her behind." I told Kristy.

"We can't leave her behind, you idiot; she would've made us all miss seeing Dad. Sometimes, it's just not worth it." Anna stuck out her tongue at me as she skipped ahead of us.

While Mom took care of the boat rental, I walked to the water's edge. The cool water lapped over my feet as lake currents shone in the morning sun. I shaded my eyes to study the cliffs more closely. Ropes crisscrossed the surface as climbers clambered over the cliffs. Their voices carried across the lake. We loaded into the row boat, and stroked across the cool, smooth expanse to the meet-up place, and waited. Anna made us sing Row, Row, Row your Boat a million times.

Mom pointed to a small rocky shore, "That's where Dad is supposed to meet us, now we just have to pick out which climber is him!"

Every time we saw someone on a cliff above us, we would shade our eyes to study their movements and see if we could recognize Dad. For a long time though, he was MIA. Soon; hot, sunburned and bored, Kristy and I started teasing Anna.

"Anna is a banana, who likes to be called Anna fofana banana," Kristy sang at the top of her lungs. Anna hated when we rhymed her name with banana.

"I am not a banana, you stupid Kristy," Anna yelled, standing up with her hands on her hips. The boat rocked, nearly tipping everyone into the water.

"Stop it! Anna, sit down!" Mom yelled and, pointing to the cliff, shouted out, "There he is! I see his yellow shirt!"

We all looked up; Dad was high on the rocks looking strong, climbing down towards an overhang. We watched as he slowly made his way down a steep cliff, carefully selecting his footing, grabbing bits and pieces of nature to hold on to. He inched down the rock face toward us, towards the lake. My mouth was dry as I watched him. It was still a long way down. Heart pounding, I closed my eyes, willing him to get to the bottom quickly.

"Jim!" my mother cried out.

My eyes snapped open just in time to see Dad's foot slip. He swung out over the cliff, dangling briefly before finding his footing again. Sighing with relief, I clutched the seat and forced myself to watch. My relief was short-lived; soon he was sliding again. Frantically, Dad clawed at the cliffs, grabbing at branches, rocks, anything.

I cried out when he hit his head on a rock; I reached out to catch him, but he continued to plummet down.

My mother covered Anna's eyes. My eyes stayed glued to Dad, willing him to find a place to catch hold.

"Please Daddy, please, grab on, please Daddy, please!" I begged him as he continued to plunge toward the lake.

"Stop! Stop!" Kristy yelled, her hand held out like a policeman stopping traffic.

Fighting hard to catch hold of something, he hit one last cliff, bounced off the edge, and fell a long way down into the water.

I heard his screams.

The few seconds it took for him to fall, and our collective lives to end, felt like hours. The screaming continued after he disappeared. Mom and Anna sat motionless, Mom's hands still over Anna's eyes; both were crying.

Kristy crawled over to Mom, bumped her aside, picked up the oars and started rowing. Her frantic efforts were uneven. My head spun and my stomach lurched as we turned in circles.

"Julia, stop!" my mom demanded. The screaming stopped, I rubbed my raw throat, and saliva gathered in my mouth, reluctant to go past the sandpaper that was my throat.

Taking the oars from Kristy, Mom took us to where Dad fell. "No, please. No!" Mom pleaded. We all stared into the dark water, except for Anna, who covered her eyes with one hand and one ear with the other.

When we reached the spot, Kristy stood and jumped in. "Come on Julia, we have to find him!" she yelled, as she disappeared below the surface.

I stood, lost my balance, and fell in with a big splash. It was cold and cloudy; I couldn't see anything but my sister swimming nearby. I spun around in the murky lake, feeling for my dad, but my hands remained empty. No matter how far I swam down, I couldn't reach the bottom. It was cool and silent as I went farther, my ears popped, and my lungs pleaded for air, forcing me back to the surface.

"Girls, come back!" my mother begged. Leaning over the side, she put her hands in the water and started scooping water into the boat, as if she could rescue him one handful at a time.

I took a big breath and went back under. In the quiet, I listened for Dad, but the lake would not give him back. Coming up for air again, I took big breaths as my head spun and I swallowed the murky water. Spitting it out, I clung to the side of the boat. Kristy was off in the distance, diving down again and again, coming up empty-handed and gasping for air.

"Get in, Julia!" Mom cried, swiping at her tears, as she grabbed my arm.

"No, not without Dad. Help us!"

A dinghy with an older couple pulled up beside us

"We saw what happened, what can we do?"

"Help us find our dad!" I yelled, "He's in here somewhere!" I wrestled out of my mother's grasp and plunged down, kicking off the side of the boat. Waves pushed me back and forth as the man jumped in to help.

Kristy kicked me as she swam past. "I can't find him!" she panted, taking huge gulps of air. Her hair was plastered to her face and her shirt was up over her bathing suit top. Yanking on her shirt, she pushed the hair out of her face.

"Keep trying!" she yelled at me, as she dove again into the dark depths that had swallowed him.

The man surfaced and treaded water next to us, "I can't see anything down there!" he said, coughing.

"The rangers are coming!" the woman yelled from the dinghy, as the sound of motors filled the air.

Exhausted and shivering, Kristy and I clung to our boat and watched a ranger talk to the older woman before one ranger slipped into the water and swam over to us.

"I'm going to help you two into the boat now," he said, "We will look for your dad."

I felt myself being lifted out of the water, flopping into the bottom of the boat like a dead fish. I lay, limbs paralyzed, staring at the sky, trying to breathe, and keep my broken heart from bursting from my chest. I closed my eyes, hoping this was all a bad, bad dream, opening them when Kristy landed on top of me.

"Julia, we can't give up, let's go back in; come on!" She got to her knees and tried to jump back in, but exhaustion overtook her and she fell back.

Sitting up, I tucked my arms in my shirt to warm myself, and watched the men. Anna jumped on both of us, clinging to us and crying while Mom sat silently staring into the dark depths.

Another ranger approached us, his boat gently bumping ours. "Ma'am?" the ranger called, "ma'am?" he repeated. The third time, Mom turned to look at him. "I'd like to take you to shore; we'll continue the search." He tied our boat to his.

"No!" Mom protested, trying to row back to the spot. "We'll wait here. He'll be back shortly," she said calmly, scanning the area as if Dad had stepped out for a gallon of milk.

My mouth dropped open as I stared at her; she had clearly lost her mind! "Find him!" I yelled at the ranger.

"Mom! Cut it out!" Kristy pleaded with her, as two men disappeared under the water to continue the search.

"No!" Mom yelled again, but her voice was drowned out by the motor. Mom continued to row against the pull of the motor boat, struggling to get back to where Dad had disappeared, even as they towed us farther and farther from him. Eventually she gave in, but even then, still continued to move the paddles above the water in a rowing motion. As the ranger towed us, we stared at the spot that swallowed him. By the time we got to shore we were facing backwards, focused on where we saw him for the last time.

The ranger tried to help us out of the boat, but none of us moved. We just stared backwards, our eyes fixed on that one horrible spot on the lake. After a few attempts, one of the rangers grabbed the gunwale and pulled our rowboat out of the water, leaving us in it.

"We'll keep looking for him as long as it takes," a ranger said gently, as he left us to our misery. "Move along folks," he added, addressing the people surrounding us who had gathered on the beach to watch the rescue.

They ignored him. People crowded up against us offering comfort or pestering us with questions until the ranger came back with some stakes and yellow caution tape, clearing a square of safety for us.

We sat, waited, hoped, eyes glued to the lake, ignoring the heat and the sun beating down on us. Gawkers still pushed against the yellow tape, pointing and talking. I tried to block out the incessant chatter. They were all talking about Dad and they needed to shut up.

I put my hands over my ears, but my eyes could not be torn away from "The Spot" They dried out from staring, looking, searching, for any sign of him. Each blink, felt like glass etching the view of him falling into my mind's eye.

I covered Anna with a towel as she lay across mom's lap. Kristy and I curled up in the bottom of the boat, water soaking into my clothes, my skin. Mom sat upright, clutching our damp shirts in her hands as if to prevent us from disappearing. Anna eventually fell asleep, clutching a sodden stuffy. I found myself holding one, too. Kristy covered her head with her shirt; I watched as her legs turned pink in the sun, but couldn't find my voice to say anything about it. Mom and I just stared across the lake. My skin roasted, sweat ran freely down my back and my mouth was as dry as the desert. Once in a while, I would see someone up on the cliffs, climbing down, and hope would fill my soul that it was Dad, and this had all been just a bad dream. The activity of the rangers, jumping into the water to continue the search across the lake, kept it real, though, and my heart continued to drum with dread, fear, and worse—the truth.

"He'll be right back. He'll be right back. He'll be right back," my mother mumbled over and over as the hours stretched. Looking at her, as she stared at the water, I wondered what she saw, and what was going through her head. I tried more than once to get her to let go of my shirt, but she held firm, pulling us toward her. Tears rolled down my cheeks until the day's heat and the sun dried up all the moisture in my body.

We sat all afternoon in the boat until the ranger came back to us. I was starving. Kristy rubbed her burnt legs. The beach had started to empty. Nearby, I could smell hot dogs roasting. The sounds of laughter and people splashing in the water echoed off the rocks. The sun dipped below the highest cliff and I shivered as the air began to cool.

"Ma'am," the ranger said, "we are going to take you to one of our cabins for the night." The ranger pointed to a row of cabins lining the shore. Mom looked at him, eyes unfocused.

"Did you find Jim?" she asked. "Will he be joining us?"

"No, ma'am, we haven't found him yet," the ranger replied. "We'll look again in the morning."

Gently, the ranger helped us out of the boat, one by one. My legs were stiff, my back hurt. I didn't want to go, and wasn't sure my heart would keep beating if I did. Kristy stumbled on the soft sand; Anna refused to walk.

"Come on, Anna," I urged, "aren't you hungry?" She stood there with her thumb in her mouth, the bag of stuffies wet and forgotten in the bottom of the boat. Picking up the bag, I turned around so Anna could climb on my back, and said, "Jump on."

Hoisting Anna up, my sunburned skin screamed in protest as she clung to my back. We made a trail of despair toward the cabin as we wove through a crowd of people, beach towels, and overflowing trash cans. Some averted their eyes. Others watched us, like rubberneckers, trying to get a better look at a car wreck. I heard questions being flung at us, but stared straight ahead. One woman reached out to touch Mom's arm. Mom just slapped the hand away and continued on.

The screen door of the cabin creaked as it opened, greeting us with the smell of mildew and burnt logs. The ranger made us peanut butter and jelly sandwiches and helped us make up squeaky bunks for the night. As we sat around the small kitchen table, nibbling on our sandwiches, Anna voiced what we were all thinking.

"Where's Daddy?"

As those words hung in the air, Kristy's head hit the table with a loud thump, her wailing filled the room. Mom stared at the ceiling as if the answer lay in the rafters. I stared at my sister, not sure what to say. I rubbed her back as she looked at me with her big blue eyes, a jelly ring circling her mouth.

"They, they are looking for him," I stuttered, before a sob burst from my throat. Kristy jumped up, running into the bedroom; I followed. I heard Anna's little voice talking to my mother, a chair scrape the floor and a door shut.

Usually my sister and I would fight over the top bunk, but this time Kristy fell into the lower bunk and sobbed herself to sleep. Feeling no sense of victory, I slowly climbed to the top bunk and settled down onto the thin mattress. The hot air in the cabin closed in on me as I tossed and turned, the bed squeaking and dust puffing out of the mattress with every turn.

Sitting up, I stifled a scream; what if Dad made it back to camp and we weren't there? I jumped down and stood at the screen door, peering out in the darkness for any sign of him. I stepped outside, ready to find our campsite, before realizing I had no idea where it was in the light, let alone in the dark. Dad would be frantic if he couldn't find us.

Slipping into the darkness, I walked toward the lake. Boats were scattered across the beach, ready to meet the dawn and start the search again. Climbing in one, I wished I could go out and keep looking. The sounds of the night echoed off the rocks. All the smells and sounds that were so friendly just last night felt like the enemy tonight. It meant life was going on without my Dad in it, and that was not how it was supposed to be.

"Dad, where are you?" I whispered to the night air, "Please be okay, please come back to us." Walking back into the cabin, I stood over Kristy's bed, shaking her foot.

"Kristy, wake up! What if Dad gets back to camp and we aren't there?"

"Huh?" Kristy blinked several times as she tried to wake up. Her glassy, blood shot eyes stared back at me, before she shook her head slowly and laid her head back down on the flat, musty pillow.

"Go back to bed, Julia. He's not there.

"How do you know?"

She sat up; "You saw him fall, he's not sitting at our camp fire wondering where we are!" Her voice escalated, "He's gone, Julia, he's dead!"

My hand hit her cheek before I knew what I was doing. Kristy fell back on her bed, crying. I slowly climbed back to my bunk, feeling the sand grind into my sunburn.

For a long time, I refused to close my eyes, fearful of seeing the image of Dad's fall replay over and over again. When my eyes started to shut, I pried them open with my fingers, refusing to give in to the nightmare that awaited me. I spent the sleepless night planning what Dad and I would do together when he came back safe and sound. I fantasized about hiking to the top of the cliffs with him, laughing at the fools who risked their lives to climb them. He would promise me then to never, ever risk his life again, then we would take the trail back to our happy life. As I lay in the darkness, I listened for him, his footsteps, his voice, anything to reassure me that everything was going to be okay.

*   *   *

Eventually, I must have dozed off, because I jumped up when the screen door slammed. A pale light trickled in through the window, signaling early morning. Hopping down, I looked out the cabin door; Mom was sitting on the beach, knees pulled up to her chin, rocking back and forth. Slowly, I walked toward her. The sand was cool on my feet and the sun was just above the horizon. It was a beautiful sunrise. I soaked it in for a minute before the full impact of Dad's fall crashed over me again.

I collapsed beside Mom, pulling my knees up, too. She looked at me briefly but re-focused her vision back to the spot on the lake. Drawing circles in the cool sand, I waited for my mother to say something, anything; she remained silent.

Another squeak of the screen door brought Kristy and Anna to us. Kristy carried Anna and her bag of stuffies. They were eating peanut butter and jelly sandwiches. Kristy pulled two sandwiches out of the bag and handed one to Mom and me. I took a bite of mine, watching as Mom's slipped from her hand as if she had no strength to hold it. I picked it up, blew off the sand as best I could and handed it back to her. She took it, setting it in the sand.

We returned to the roped off section of the beach, as the rangers launched boats into the water. They motored across the lake, taking turns diving. Anna was humming loudly with her hands over her eyes.

"Shut up!" I yelled at her, she burst into tears. Watching the tears roll down her cheeks, I didn't feel sorry for her. She was still here alive while Dad was out there somewhere cold and alone!

Time passed slowly as people walked by with their dogs, or walked around us to set up for a day at the beach. Coolers and umbrellas soon littered the sand, butting up against our square of safety, as if we were hogging the prime spot.

A shout came from the across the lake, voices echoed loudly through the early morning air. Mom stood up; we all stood up. Kristy stood on the sandwich, grinding it further into the sand. Mom walked to the edge of the water; soon she was ankle deep, then knee deep. I ran in, pulling her back from walking to Dad.

"Mom, stop!" She tried to break my grip, to shuffle forward; Kristy dragged her back to the shore. Anna covered her eyes and I began praying to a God I didn't know very well.

Maybe God could help! What did I know, though? We got together on Christmas Eve and Easter, but otherwise usually went our separate ways.

Knees! I remembered, you are supposed to pray on your knees. Not knowing the mechanics of why, I couldn't risk it. I fell to my knees ignoring the sand grinding into them. Clasping my hands together, low in my lap, I prayed, hoping I was doing it right.

"Dear God, please, please, please, let Dad be alive. I will take him anyway you want me to have him, I am begging you, I will do anything, give you anything if only he comes back to us."

Trying to think of what I could give God in return, my eyes fell on my little sister, Anna. She was innocently sitting in the sand, Hoppy clutched in one hand, her other hand over her eyes. Sand was stuck to her hands and legs. Her hair had been in pigtails yesterday, today, they were sad tails dragging along her little shoulders. Only feeling a little ashamed, I offered her up to him in my prayer for a miracle.

"Dear God, I know she doesn't look like much," I glanced back at her, "but she is very sweet, she loves animals, she could be the pet greeter. She would love that. I just want Dad back!"

Across the lake, the rangers loaded something onto a floating stretcher attached to a boat. They covered it with a blue tarp. I prayed even harder.

A ranger approached us, startling me as my focus was on waiting for the heavens to open up and my sister to be lifted up in trade for Dad returning to us. So far, she was just sitting there with her eyes covered, rocking. Glaring at her did not seem to be speeding up the transaction. The ranger took Mom aside; I inched closer to hear him.

"Ma'am, can I speak to you, please?" Mom looked at him with a vacant stare.

"It's about your husband; can I speak to you privately, please?"

Mom looked at him, "You found him? Is he coming home?"

The ranger turned to us, "Girls, can you please wait in the cabin while I talk to your mother?"

Kristy and I froze, our eyes locked; if this was news we weren't supposed to hear, it had to be bad.

"Did you find him? Say what you have to say, my kids aren't going anywhere," Mom screeched.

"I really think it would be best if the girls went into the cabin," the ranger tried again. I stood firm. I wasn't going anywhere. Kristy stepped from foot to foot, walking in place as if undecided on whether to go or stay. Anna was just humming like she always did. Mom stared past the ranger, her hair was flattened to her head, her shirt tucked into one side of her shorts, and her eyes fixed across the lake.

"The girls stay."

The ranger knelt down in front of my mother and spoke in a low voice; I had to strain to hear.

"We found him."

Mom's head whipped around toward the ranger; she smiled. "Oh, good! You found Jim." she exclaimed. "We can go home now, girls." She started to call us.

"Ma'am" the ranger interrupted, "Jim did not survive the fall, I am very sorry."

Mom and I collapsed on the sand at the same time. Crawling on my hands and knees, I went over to her; Kristy followed. We sat on either side of Mom while the ranger spoke. I strained to hear him over Kristy's loud sobs.

"We are bringing him to shore now. I think it's best if you all wait in the cabin," he said.

The window of opportunity for my miracle trade was closing, yet Anna was still here. The ranger tried to help Mom to her feet.

"We will wait right here," Mom said firmly, yanking her arm out of his hand.

"Ma'am?" the rangers asked, "Can we take the girls, at least?"

"No, they will want to see their dad." She shaded her eyes and watched the boat come into shore. The ranger ran his fingers through his hair.

Kristy got up, "Come on Julia, Anna, let's go!"

"No!" I yelled at her, "Dad is not dead! He is coming back to us!" My mother's head bobbed up and down in agreement.

"Julia, you heard what he said," Kristy sobbed, "Dad is not coming back to us! We shouldn't see this!"

"Then go!" I screamed at her.

Kristy looked lost for a second, then picked up Anna and her bag of stuffies and ran to the cabin. Two fell out along the way, marking the trail. Still hoping for my miracle trade, I stayed on the beach.

"Dad for Anna. Dad for Anna," I quietly pleaded. Mom took my hand as we watched the boat come to shore. Her hand was cold and bony; I tried to imagine they were Dad's big warm hands, hoping with all my heart I would feel them hugging me one more time.

A ranger pulled the boat and the stretcher onto the shore. A shoe stuck out of the bottom of the tarp; I recognized Dad's hiking boot. Falling back, crab crawling backwards, I used my hands and feet to propel me away from the blue tarp and its unwelcome contents.

"No! No, no!" I moaned, as I backed away from the collapse of my family.

The ranger helped Mom up, leading her over to the covered bundle that I refused to believe was my dad. Slowly, the ranger peeled back a small piece of the tarp. Mom fell to her knees.

"Jim!" Falling across the tarp, she shook him.

"Jim, wake up! Please wake up!" she begged. "Oh, God! No, no, no, please Jim, no" She collapsed next to the stretcher, keening in a high pitched voice.

An unknown force lifted me to my feet and pushed me over to stand behind Mom. I didn't want to see, I wanted to run, but my shaky legs planted themselves behind my parents. There was only a small opening in the tarp where a face was showing. It looked like Dad, but blue and swollen. Turning away, I retched, the sour remains of my sandwich filled my mouth. My world started to spin; Dad's face was the last thing I saw before it all went black.

*     *     *

For a long time, whenever I closed my eyes, I saw my dad falling. Seared into my mind's eye was the sight of him hitting the cliff, bouncing off and falling into the water, screaming until he disappeared.

Later, I changed the image to one of him standing on top of the highest cliff, then performing a perfect swan dive, except when he broke form to wave one last goodbye to us, before disappearing without a splash into the still, cool water.

*The End is an excerpt from Linda Meyer's novel, Swan Dive.*

## A Week in the Life of an Ordinary Teenage Store Clerk

### Mark Ballweg

### *Tuesdays are normally uneventful*

Tyler rang up the order. "That'll be eight dollars and fifty cents, Mrs. Mackenzie."

The elderly woman, a regular to anyone who frequented the convenience store, smiled at the clerk as the clasp on her purse opened. A few bills and coins floated over gray-tiled flooring and scuffed the counter to hover nonchalantly besides the cash register. As if a string was cut, the money suddenly dropped from the sky into the clerk's already outstretched hand. The radius of her attribute wasn't more than a few feet, a fact Tyler had learned to account for.

"Shame you're stuck inside today," Mrs. Mackenzie said with a smile as Tyler counted the coins. She turned and pointed shakily past the shelves of dried fruit and batteries, and through the clear glass windows of the store. It was a bright and sunny April day, with just the right amount of clouds to add dimension to a sky so uniformly blue that it'd otherwise look flat. Tyler followed her gaze and smiled while letting out a sigh.

"I would if I could," he replied, his shoulders slumping. Tyler held out a receipt for Mrs. Mackenzie, extending his arm a little more than he did for other customers until he felt the now familiar tug of power. The receipt floated into her bag with ease, and she closed it. "But it certainly has brightened up in here since you walked in," he added with a grin.

"Oh you," Mrs. Mackenzie said, a touch of red spreading across her wrinkled skin. "You're too much today." The woman grinned back as the plastic parcel Tyler had bagged for her drifted beside her, invisible hands tying the handles into a knot. She turned and, with the bag bobbing comfortably behind her, Mrs. Mackenzie waved goodbye as she walked through the doors. They opened automatically, as if she had activated the motion sensor, but Tyler knew better. For all his personal indulgences, Mr. Walsh hadn't invest—

"Shipment arrived," a gruff voice announced through the radio attached to Tyler's shirt, snapping him from his thoughts. "Remember to take inventory before stocking this time."

"Right away, Mr. Walsh," Tyler replied to the empty room. His boss, known for being one of the most gifted technopaths in town, was also a renowned agoraphobic. At first, Tyler had found the ghostly presence disconcerting, but Tyler needed a job, so he figured he could learn to live with it. He was right—his boss's absent omnipresence became a surprisingly comfortable constant in his life. Tyler still didn't know if Mr. Walsh was worried about the government tracking him, or if he just didn't like going outside . . . all Tyler really knew was that the man was there when he arrived and stayed after he left, spending his days and nights in the backroom locked behind an impressively intimidating door, keeping an eye and ear to what went on in his store through the various cameras and radio transmitters scattered throughout.

Tyler pictured Mr. Walsh in his above-ground bunker wearing camouflage and a helmet, his face locked in consternation. He had never even seen what the man looked like, a fact that Tyler mused on as he loaded boxes of deodorant and individually packaged cheeses onto the handcart.

Changing gears, Tyler began to play his favorite work-game "What's in the box?" The game had been born out of his boss's desire to save money by bundling items to reduce shipping costs, which resulted in outrageous combinations. As often as he played, Tyler rarely hit the mark, and he wasn't sure he ever wanted to be right.

*That's when I'll know I've been working here too long.*

Just as he finished stocking the last of the cheeses, the door opened for another regular, Hector Perry. Hector wasn't a man easily forgotten; he weighed almost three hundred pounds, had a balding head, and sported a pair of petite, bright pink pixie wings on the center of his back. Unfortunately, they were mostly aesthetic. To actually fly, Hector required a synthetic enzyme found only in specially manufactured foods. Even then, most contained such a trace amount he rarely left the ground for more than a few seconds.

Hector walked around an aisle or two, touching this and that, before letting out a long, almost practiced groan.

Sensing his cue, Tyler rose from his crouched position in the dairy section and said, "Hey Hector. Everything alright?"

The man let out another groan, his paper-thin wings drooping. Not for the first time, Tyler wondered if he bought specially made shirts, or just ripped holes through standard ones. "Tyler, you wouldn't *believe* the day I've been having."

In truth, the answer to Hector's altitude problem came in the form of Ciento Veinte Caballos (De Fuerza), an energy drink that flooded the market a few years ago. The stuff claimed to boost the body's efficiency by 120% but, from what Tyler understood, it tasted like day-old yogurt dipped in rusted steel. It had the exact enzyme Hector needed to obtain flight, but also contained about 1000% of one's daily-recommended dose of sugar. For health reasons, it had immediately been banned in North America, but that didn't stop its popularity or mass consumption. The company simply moved to Sweden where the rules were a bit looser.

Tyler's boss was not one to let legalities stand in the way of profits, especially for a long time client like Hector, who had frequented the store since well before the drink was released. Because the drink's parent company also sold a cheap brand of almonds, Mr. Walsh had no problem using his technopathic skills to subterfuge the system and include a case every now and then for the man (it was paid for, Mr. Walsh assured Tyler).

Unfortunately, this provided a Catch-22 for Hector, since the drink that now granted him flight increased his girth, which meant he needed even greater amounts the next time. Tyler could tell Hector was very self-conscious about his weight from the way he seemed to glance around the store to see if the judgmental stares he felt were real or imagined. Regardless, Tyler felt his own share of shame for being part of the cycle.

Hector's wings fluttered a few times unconsciously. The effort moved the air like a fan set to a low speed. "What happened today?" Tyler asked, when Hector didn't begin on his own.

"Well . . ." Hector started, leaning on the aisle display and causing it to bend only a little, "I woke up this morning thinking, 'Okay, enough is enough! Today's the day I finally get my life in order. I'll start by taking a quick bike ride,' but, of course, my tires are flat on account of that cold snap we had the other night."

"Weather has been crazy," Tyler nodded in agreement.

"Right? So I say, 'That's okay, I'll go for a walk.' But, naturally, I forgot my running shoes were at the drycleaners. Anyway, I was sitting in my room, trying to think of a way to get some exercise, when I saw a commercial on TV for one of those high-protein low-fat something-or-other bars. Please tell me you've got them in stock?"

"Sure do." Tyler walked the man over to the third aisle and gestured to the stack.

"Perfect! I'll grab a few of these and be on my way, then."

As Hector picked up a handful and made his way to the cashier's counter, Tyler knew it was his turn. The reason varied from visit to visit, but there was an unspoken rule between the two to always have Tyler make the first move. Conversationally, Tyler mentioned, "Oh man, I totally forgot about that. Mr. Walsh is going to kill me.”

“What’s that?” Hector asked, curious.

“Well, you know how Mr. Walsh likes to order from exotic places, right?”

“Of course, he has some of the rarest inventory in town.”

“Yeah, well, some of the websites aren’t in English. And I’m clearly a few bristles short of a broom, because I keep accidently setting up automatic-reordering on this stupid drink from Sweden. So we keep getting cases, and I can’t get anyone to buy them! Now, Mr. Walsh says if I don’t sell them soon, it’ll come out of my paycheck!”

Hector let out a gasp. “He can’t do that!”

In response, Tyler simply shrugged. “What can I do? He’s the boss, and it was my mistake.”

“Not right, not right,” Hector replied, shaking his head in disapproval. After a few seconds of heavy thinking, Hector said, “Tell you what, since you’ve been such a good friend listening to me complain today, what say I take a case off your hands? I do like to support local businesses, after all.”

## _Wednesdays are the best_

Tyler stopped sweeping to glance again at the clock section of the store. It was almost time. He resumed his cleaning, brushing repeatedly over the same spot, which was starting to cause some wear on the floor. He had to look busy, but not _too_ busy. That would defeat the entire point. It was a delicate balance to look like he was doing enough to be important, but not _so_ important that he couldn’t be interrupted from his task for a short conversation about life, or school, or—

"Tyler?" The voice behind him froze him in place as the awaited recognition set in.

It was a voice you could hear once and then pick out in a crowd years later. It was the sound of angels singing, of babies smiling, of a full orchestra reaching the climax of a song, of—

"You . . . alright?" she asked.

"Jackie!" Tyler shouted her name as he spun around on the broom. Before him stood the most beautiful girl in the world. And, in her case, it wasn't an overstatement. Standing at five-and-a-half feet tall with black shoulder-length hair, literally anyone who so much as glanced at her gaped in awe. Man, woman, child, animal, probably even inanimate objects too. It didn't matter. This was her gift, her attribute, her life. She was beautiful, and Tyler was only too happy to spend a few minutes with her every week.

"Sorry, I didn't mean to startle you." Jackie awkwardly rubbed at one of her arms. Today she graced the world with an elegant forest green blouse, with sleeves that flared at the elbows, and waves of ruffles that decorated the hem. On anyone else, it would have been just a green shirt, but on Jackie it looked like a hand-tailored masterpiece.

Tyler felt himself staring, and made an effort to turn his attention back to his sweeping. "What? Me? No, sorry, just got lost in thought a little; didn't even hear you come in." *At least that last part was true.*

Jackie smiled at him, and he could feel the warmth even as he stared down at the floor. He stopped sweeping and composed himself as he leaned the broom against the wall. Immediately, he wished he had held onto it—without the broom, he felt awkward as he felt his hands fall to his side, then cross at his chest, before finally resting with his thumbs hooked into one pocket and a belt loop.

"What can I help you with today?" he asked, shifting once again to place one hand in his pocket while the other leaned along the wall.

It looked just as awkward as it felt.

In response, Jackie let out a giggle that almost made him melt. "I was just trying to find some hair clips. Mine keep breaking on me. Not sure why."

"Yeah, we have some that you'd like that are pretty cheap," Tyler said before his brain caught up to his mouth and mentally slapped it for speaking without permission. He quickly followed up with, "Not that I think you buy cheap things! I just meant that if you're going through them so much then these won't break the bank. Not that I don't think your modeling career pays you enough to buy something better. I know you have plenty of money. Not that I care about your money! I just. . . ." His brain strangled his vocal cords to a halt as he let his head hang in despair. Left hand extended, he said, "Fifth aisle over, next to the foldable sporks and combs."

"Thanks," she said, sliding over to the appropriate row. She sorted through the display case, humming to herself, and picked out a few colors and styles. "It's not the money, you know," she said suddenly. "Sure, there might be more expensive ones out there that are more durable, like the ones all the famous movie stars and heroes wear. But those just feel so . . . fake, you know? These feel more real, more honest."

"Plus, I have it on good authority these aren't made by child laborers in Canada," Tyler said, picking his head up and moving behind the register.

"Oh my god, I heard about that on the news! I'm just glad the heroes could arrive and put those people behind bars where they belong."

"That's a terrible thing to say! I mean, they're just children," Tyler chided with a grin.

"Oh, shut up," Jackie stuck her tongue out at him as she placed a new clip in her hair. It had small black butterflies with a few gems that glittered like stars in the night sky. "So, how do I look?" She stepped towards him and struck a pose, head twisting so her hair could fall over half her face, her uncovered eyebrow raised in an amused look.

"W-What, that?" Tyler answered, breathlessly. His mouth got very dry, and his heart threatened to burst from his chest. "I mean, I guess it works. If you're into that kind of thing."

Jackie let out a loud laugh, a small snort sneaking through as she clamped her hands over her nose. Despite her evident horror, she still let out a few more laughs. "Oh Tyler, you're hysterical. I almost would have bought that apathetic routine if your face hadn't gotten all red there."

Tyler felt his face burn hotter than a chili pepper as he started to ring up her items. "Yeah well, you know . . . I . . ." His brain struggled for control as he sounded out each next word carefully, as if he had never said them before. "You know, *ahem*, Jackie, I don't know if you'd be, well, you know, interested, at all, but, well, there's this new Viking movie that seems pretty cool, and—"

A sudden melody started to play from Jackie's purse. "Oh, hold that thought," she said as she placed her bag on the counter and fished out her phone. "Hey Shawn," she answered, taking a few steps away in an attempt at privacy.

As she spoke, Tyler shook his head clear and rang up her items, giving her the celebrity discount that Mr. Walsh demanded apply to her, despite her constant arguments against it.

"But we were supposed to get dinner tonight with my parents," she said into the phone, voice quieter. "I know but . . . I heard you but . . . Alright . . . Yeah, that's fine . . . We still on for Saturday? . . . Okay, great. See you later. Love you."

Jackie hung up the phone and made her way back to the counter. "Sorry about that. What were you saying?"

"Hmm?" Tyler questioned. "Me, no, I wasn't saying anything. You were saying something about . . . the . . . thing. . . ." His voice trailed off, eyes darting everywhere but to her.

"Right. . . ." Jackie placed her money on the counter, neither knowing where to pick up their conversation, as Tyler completed the transaction.

Leaving the clip in her hair, Jackie waited for a few more seconds before finally saying, "Alright, well, I've got to get to the studio. I'll see you in Chemistry tomorrow?"

"It's a date." Tyler's brain threw up its arms in defeat as he watched Jackie glide out the door.

### *Thursdays are almost bearable*

"Swoosh! Another point for me!"

A small projectile arced high in the air before landing with a small thud. The remnants of past throws lay scattered on the floor around it.

"Would you stop throwing that crap?" Tyler scolded. His best friend, Mike, was sitting on a chair behind the register, feet up in the air with a half-filled box of individually-packaged moist towelettes beside him. The other half lay strewn about the store in accordance with whatever point system Mike had concocted this visit. Apparently, tonight he was winning. "You know I have to clean those up, right?"

"Oh, come on, you know I'll help you." Mike threw another one that bounced off Tyler's head. "Bonus point!"

"I know you'll *say* you will, but something will conveniently come up and get you out of it."

"I *am* a popular person," Mike grinned.

"Come on man, look at this place. What would I say if someone walked in here right now?"

"You'd say, 'Hi sir, you must be lost. What reputable establishment were you looking for tonight so that I might give you better directions?'"

Tyler rolled his eyes and started to pick up the thrown items. When he was almost done, arms full of the tiny squares, his body let out an uncontrollable hiccup that caused him to drop them all. He stood there, arms empty, anger rising, before looking up and glaring daggers at his friend.

"Yes?" Mike asked innocently. "Oh, sure, because every time you hiccup it has to be my fault?"

"If the cape fits . . ." Tyler said, bending down to gather them again. As he stood, another projectile went flying over his head. "I swear I'm going to tell Mr. Walsh to stop letting you in here."

"I've tried," a voice crackled through the speaker on Tyler's shoulder. "But evidently his attribute can penetrate even my thick walls."

Mike let out a cheer and gave a thumbs up to the closest camera. "Couldn't resist. You know I like you,

Walsh. You're good people."

"However, if he doesn't make a purchase or stop preventing my employee from working, I can have his car towed."

This got Mike's attention, and in a flash he was by Tyler's side. "Buddy, my man, come on now, you're working too hard. Why don't you let me help you out a bit?"

"How terribly kind of you," Tyler sneered.

Mike placed a hand to his chest. "I do it from the goodness of my heart."

The two got to work straightening out the store. It was close to eleven, the end of Tyler's shift. Thursdays were usually long and boring, at least they were until Mike arrived to crash the last hour or so.

"Speaking of altruism, how are your folks?"

Mike shrugged. "Oh, you know. Saving cats from burning houses and people who are stuck up trees. Or something like that; I don't listen much."

"It doesn't show."

"My old man says he's taking me out on patrol with him this weekend."

"Yeah?" Tyler raised an eyebrow. "Is that a punishment or reward?"

"Bit of both. I think he's desperate to find a productive use of my attribute. I can't stop bad guys by flying or running fast, or by jumping over buildings or stopping trains with my mind, but hey, I can aggravate their diaphragms better than anyone, so I've got to be useful. But, you know. Not as useful as my dad flying in and actually stopping the villain and saving the day."

"So you're . . . bait?" Tyler asked.

"I like to think of myself as slightly better than that!" Mike paused. "You know, like a really attractive decoy."

"So a temptation?"

"More of a diversion."

"Like a fake?"

"Façade is better."

"What about a lure?" Mr. Walsh asked.

"No, see, now we're back to bait again." Mike let out a breath. "Well, whatever I am, I'm sure I'll hate it."

"That's the spirit!" Tyler said, clapping his friend on the shoulder. "If it makes you feel any better, I'm stuck working this weekend."

"With any luck, someone'll try to rob the place and we can hang out."

Tyler smiled. "I'd like that."

"I wouldn't," Mr. Walsh countered.

In response, Mike picked the speaker off Tyler's shirt and threw it across the room. Then, remembering Mr. Walsh's threat, ran after it in alarm.

### *Fridays suck*

Tyler ran through the doors, backpack in one arm and vest half on.

"Sorry!" he shouted to the store. It was empty, with the day employee, Rick, having left when his shift ended at three. He glanced at the clock—3:27pm. "Curses," he cursed.

"I heard that," Mr. Walsh said through the speaker at the counter. Tyler walked over and pinned it to his shirt. "You know I had to turn away five customers already."

"I know; I'm sorry." Tyler rubbed his hands over his face. "I got held up at school. It won't happen again."

There were a few seconds of silence before Mr. Walsh asked, "Do you want to talk about it?"

Tyler let out a laugh. If there was one thing Mr. Walsh hated more than leaving his specially made room, it was talking about people's problems. "No thanks, Mr. Walsh. But . . . thanks for asking?"

He could all but hear his boss' sigh of relief. "Anytime. When you're settled, the new shipments of potatoes and syringes came in. Rick unloaded them from the truck and did inventory, but didn't have time to stock them."

With that, Tyler walked behind the counter to the backroom and got to work. He took a little solace in the fact that, no matter how bad things got at school, he did have this store to retreat to. Sure it was menial labor, but here, he could be . . . anyone. Just another regular working guy, eager to make a living and converse with the patrons who walk in. Here he was a nobody, which worked out well because he really wasn't anyone important outside either. At least here, he was the only one who knew that.

Then the doors opened.

Four rowdy teenage boys entered the store, laughing to themselves. In the back room, Tyler's hands tightened on the crate he was sorting as a chill ran through his spine. He recognized the voices. Soon enough, he heard banging and crashing, and winced as various bags popped and cans crashed. Tyler peeked his head around the corner to confirm what he had feared: The Devil and his Demons had arrived.

The Devil, also known as Shawn Morris, was intimidating to say the least. No matter what he claimed, his only real attribute seemed to be a skin pigmentation change from normal to a dark crimson red, with his eyes black instead of white. That was it. Nothing impressive or shocking, given the attributes some of the rest of the world held. But, since he actually went to the gym for strength training, was a general jerk, and loaded his black hair with an inconceivable amount of gel to stylize it like horns, you *did* get the impression that he was a spawn of Satan.

His demonic minions weren't that much better. Quentin, Max, and King followed Shawn around like homeless dogs smelling food, and behaved about as well. From his hiding spot, Tyler saw Quentin turn the left side of his body invisible (a choice made by the limitation of his ability, not laziness), grab a chocolate bar from the shelf and pocket it, whistling to himself as if the cameras didn't just see a floating bar of candy. Max and Shawn rifled through the liquor area, while at the front, King, with his two antennae moving atop his head, pounded on the counter.

"Service! Service!" He slammed the counter a few more times, antennae moving in all directions. "I can sense you in the back. Come on, we've got places to be!"

Tyler let out the breath, counted a silent five, and walked out from the backroom.

"Holy Hero!" King shouted when he caught sight of Tyler. Urging the others over, he said with a laugh, "Hey guys, look who it is!" The other three stopped what they were doing and gathered around to gawk at their classmate.

"Well if it isn't Talentless Tyler," Shawn said, pushing past his cronies like a man on a mission. "What the hell are you doing here?" he snickered.

Tyler glanced down at his nametag, then to his position behind the counter, and then back up at him. "I .

. . work here," he answered carefully. He had never gotten along with these guys before, and doubted it would change now, but he still didn't want to start a fight.

"Oh, a real smart-alecky guy here," Max said, elbowing King in the ribs. Behind him, Quentin picked up a picture frame and tucked it under his jacket.

"Hey!" Tyler said to Quentin, mid-theft. "If you're going to try to steal, at least use your invisible side."

Two large, red fingers snapped in front of Tyler, shocking him back a step. "Keep your attention on me, okay Tyler?" Shawn taunted, moving in front of him to take over Tyler's entire field of vision. He liked to showcase his muscles by wearing black leather vests as often as possible, regardless of the weather. Today, he made a special effort at flexing as he pointed to his friends. Each crony lifted a case of beer onto the counter. "We'll just be taking these, if that's *alright* with you."

"Sure thing, just need to see some ID first." Tyler said with a smile. Of course, when Shawn smiled back at him, Tyler regretted it.

"For what? Water?" Shawn nudged Max forward, who touched the clear glass bottles. One by one, the dark beverage inside turned to a clear liquid. Tyler simply rolled his eyes. Max was famous at parties for this, being able to turn any liquid to water, even if it didn't stay that way for long. Apparently, it was even better when you drank it, so that when the liquid changed back inside your system, you got hit with the entire force of the alcohol at once. Shawn kept his smile of mock innocence as he passed some money across the counter.

"The boys and I are hosting a little get together tomorrow night," Shawn continued, the demons grinning behind him. "Folks are out of town all weekend, so all the cool kids and, what the hell, some of the boring ones too, are coming over. Booze, music, girls, and booze. It's gonna be a fun time."

"Sounds like it," Tyler said, head down as he watched the last of the beer turn to water.

"And don't forget the girls!" King said.

"How could I?" Shawn grinned towards Tyler. "Jackie's bringing over some of her modeling friends. You know, the hottest of the hottest. With any luck, I won't be the only one getting some that night." He started to make humping motions against the counter.

Doing his best to ignore him, Tyler counted the money, noting that it wasn't enough for one of the cases, let alone four. "If you're done violating the counter, you're a bit short."

"And you're a loser!" Shawn laughed as he bent over and grabbed two of the cases at once. "Come on guys, let's get out of here."

One by one they grabbed a case, grinning at Tyler who stood there, powerless. As Quentin passed by, he displayed his empty hands saying, "Nothing for me today, thanks."

Almost out the door, Shawn stopped and said, "Oh, and Tyler?"

"What?" he responded hesitantly.

"Be sure to give an invite to that loser friend of yours. Hiccup boy or whatever. He's usually good for a joke or two at his own expense."

The four of them laughed as they walked out the doors. Tyler allowed himself to fall back against the wall, closing his eyes and trying to steady his breathing.

"Thanks for the assist, Mr. Walsh," he said dryly.

"What's that?" a voice came from the speaker. "Sorry, had to hit the bathroom for a quick second. What'd I miss?"

### *Saturdays always bring trouble*

The television beside the cash register was tuned to the local news, and they weren't covering anything important. That worried Tyler. Saturdays always brought trouble, as everyone knew, and he had a feeling this one wouldn't be an exception. This late at night, it wasn't a question of if something would happen, but when. His worry was augmented by the knowledge that his best friend was out there putting himself at risk. Sure, his parents would be there to keep him safe, but without much actual defense to speak of from his attribute, and with his equal and opposite amount of over-confidence, Mike's odds weren't great.

Tyler heard the sound well before his mind registered what it was. A faint humming noise, and then a clap of thunder despite the clear night sky. Looking up from the TV, he peered out through the clear glass windows, trying to get a glimpse of what was happening.

A figure came crashing down in the parking lot. The shockwave knocked Tyler and a few shelves to the ground. When he regained his balance, he poked his head cautiously over the counter to see who had landed. Clad in a light blue and white costume stood a man of moderate height. He wore a helmet-like mask on his head, dark reflective plastic on the visor allowing him to see out but no one to see in. The man scanned the parking lot, then, seeing no one there to stop him, threw one hand to the side as every window on Tyler's car exploded into a fine powder.

Tyler groaned. The car wasn't even half paid off.

"Mr. Walsh..." he said quietly into the speaker.

"I see him," he responded just as softly. "Already called the Hero Hotline."

The clerk ducked, darting out of the villain's view, as he made his way to a back aisle. "Is there any chance I can come in there with you?" Tyler asked. Mr. Walsh's room had the kind of specs you wanted in this type of situation: reinforced steel, five inches thick in all directions including the ceiling and floor. Even better, it boasted at least three forms of biometric scanners that Tyler knew about to gain entry. He sensed hesitation through the static from the other side, but just when his boss might have responded, another figure landed outside.

Peeking over the aisle, Tyler let out a sigh of relief. Dressed from head to toe in a royal purple jumpsuit, the hero's muscles were all but splitting through the tight-fitted fabric of his costume. With long golden hair and boots to match, Tyler knew him as Amazinman, a local hero who was rising in fame. With him on the scene, Tyler was confidant things would be cleared up soon.

"Ha ha ha!" the villain cried out, striking a pose with his hands on his hips and chest pushed out. "It's about time a *hero* showed up. I was beginning to think no one had the guts to face me!"

"Don't think so highly of yourself, cur," Amazinman said, striking the same pose, only flexing more muscles. "We heroes were busy in the city fighting *real* threats."

The villain looked pissed, or at least as pissed as you could look with your face hidden behind a mask. "You *dare* speak that way to the great Shard?!"

"And *you* think you stand a chance against the amazing Amazinman from ToughCore©? ToughCore©, home of the top-rated get-fit-quick protein powder and supplements!"

Curious, Tyler looked closely at Amazinman's costume. Sure enough, along the boots and arms, and plastered on the square of his back, was ToughCore©'s logo. Apparently. the rumors of him selling out for any and all publicity to take him to the next level had been true.

"Bah!" Shard said, throwing out his hand at Amazinman from ToughCore©. The streetlight above the hero's head shattered into inch-long pieces of glass that were sent careening towards him with amazing speed. Instead of moving away, Amazinman from ToughCore© balled his hand into a fist and punched at the incoming projectiles. His punch stopped inches from impact, and the echoing shockwave dissolved the glass into dust. Amazinman from ToughCore© spun around, launching himself with one foot towards the villain. He punched with his other hand, but Shard had already moved aside, allowing Amazinman from ToughCore© to punch a three-foot crater into the pavement.

"Ugh!" Tyler groaned again, moving closer to get a better view. That hole was going to make parking a nightmare tomorrow. At this point, Tyler was no longer concerned for his safety. Amazinman from ToughCore© would ensure Shard was captured quickly. Instead, Tyler found himself getting closer so he would have a story to tell. After all, Jackie and everyone else were at a party, blocks away from the store. They'd have heard the noise for sure, but wouldn't be able to see anything. This was his chance to be important.

"Villain!" Amazinman from ToughCore© shouted after missing another punch and bringing down a nearby tree. "Cease this wanton destruction and come quietly, lest I be forced to use my full power!"

"I'd like to see you try!" Shard responded, moving in front of the store's windows. "If you come even one step closer, I'm going to shatter this store to rubble."

*Oh no*, Tyler thought, darting into an aisle further away from them. He started to grab whatever boxes he could find in an effort to form a barricade between the two fighters and himself.

"*I'd* like to see *you* try," Amazinman from ToughCore© taunted. "You don't have the *skill* for that!"

*Come on come on come on,* Tyler urged himself as he pulled a shelf closer. He huddled down against some canned grapes and USB drives, put his head against his knees, and braced himself.

"Fine!" Shard shouted, extending his hand to the store. "See what you think of this!"

The glass windows erupted with a deafening sound as Tyler's makeshift barricade was pressed against him.

### *Sundays are cleanup days*

Tyler raked the broom through yet another pile of broken glass. After Shard destroyed everything glass-related in the store, from the windows to the display cases in the dairy section, both villain and hero had taken to the sky, leaving a dazed but relatively unharmed Tyler to start picking up the pieces. Mr. Walsh had quickly stopped him, since the police needed to do a full write-up of the event, and the more damage there was, the more the insurance would kick in. So Tyler got to drive home in his faux-convertible, get some rest, and come in bright and early today to start the cleanup process.

He had gotten most of the larger pieces off the ground before opening the store, and seemed to be doing a good job at picking up the rest of them with his shoes. After getting stabbed for the tenth time, Tyler caved and tore open a bag of super durable, puncture-resistant rubber shoes that had come in with a shipment of Tiki torches. They were bright yellow and felt like fish, but they were thick enough that he didn't feel like he was walking on diamonds.

*Plus, it's still early enough that no one's going to see me anyway.*

"Tyler?" a voice called from the propped-open doorway. He froze. *Eventually I'll learn inner monologues get me in trouble.* Turning around, Tyler found Jackie standing there, her beauty silhouetted by the morning sun. She wore form-fitting blue jeans, a loose-fitting sweatshirt, and outlandishly large sunglasses that rested comfortably on her face.

As she attempted to take a step forward, he quickly cut in, "HATE!"

Jackie froze mid-step, eyeing him carefully. Or at least, he assumed so. He couldn't see through those dark glasses. But it *felt* like she was staring at him, so he knew he had to speak words and stop analyzing the situation, or else things would really get awkward, and he definitely didn't want that.

"I meant 'Hey,' because you're here, but 'wait' because you started moving, and, uh, glass . . . is sharp," he said pointing and reverting to the communication skills of his ancestors. "We, um, shoes! I have more of them! If you want to come in."

Jackie stood stunned and nodded silently, accepting a pair from him. They were neon red, a color that matched nothing in existence, but looked as if they had been curated just for her custom stylish look.

"I heard this place got hit bad from the fight last night," she said, walking around the store and surveying the damage. Each step she took made a *squink* sound. "I had no idea it was *this* bad."

"All things considered, it could have been worse," Tyler admitted. "All we really lost were some windows, most of the dairy line, and our stock of 1953 World's Fair glass cups. Luckily, that's all covered by insurance."

"Right. . . ." Jackie yawned gracefully as she completed her circuit, dusted off the counter and propped herself up to sit.

"Do you . . . want some coffee? I just started a pot for myself. I say just, but it was about an hour ago. I can heat it up for you."

"That'd be great," she said, smiling.

Though he tried not to seem too eager, Tyler rushed to the backroom, shoes crinkling with every step he took. At one point, he thought he heard his speaker spring to life, but it silenced itself shortly thereafter. He carefully brought back a full paper cup to Jackie. She accepted it with a smile and took off her glasses.

"Jackie!" Tyler said, partially from shock and partially in alarm. Underneath her right eye was a single cut about an inch long. The oversized glasses had covered it completely. "What happened?!"

"Oh, this?" she said, touching it gingerly. "So it is noticeable, then?"

*As noticeable as a smear on the Mona Lisa.* "What? I mean, what's noticeable?" Tyler tried to play it off but the overwhelming concern he felt for her was easily recognizable in his voice. "You know, there are healers around. They could get that fixed, make it so it doesn't even leave a scar."

"I know," Jackie responded, shrugging it off. "But, I don't know, I think I like it."

A silence grew between them as she kicked her feet anxiously against the counter with a rhythmic *tha-thud*.

"Jackie. . . ." Tyler said hesitantly. "Is everything . . . alright? Why did you come here?"

"I don't know," she said, suddenly standing in order to pace. Her feet now produced a slow tinkle-crunch-squish sound. "I guess because I knew you were the one person not at the party last night." She stopped herself, turning to add, "Not that I didn't think you should have been there—"

"It's fine," he interrupted, only a little put off.

Her shoulders slumped as she continued. "I was . . . kind of off the rails last night. Went a bit too crazy, you know? But it's like, no matter what I do, or how I act, people still see me as this, this perfect thing. It's annoying as hell!" She stopped to take an angry sip of coffee, grimacing at the taste. "I just want one person to yell at me, to say 'Stop it, you've gone too far!' or something. I know it sounds ridiculous. . . . "

"It's not that crazy," Tyler said, a bit too eager to agree.

"Yeah, well. Like I said, I went a bit nuts last night, though I doubt you'd find anyone who'd say so. And, well, one thing was leading to another, and things were starting to happen that I didn't like, and . . . anyway. I was walking out when that villain, Shart or whatever, comes crashing down into the house. Glass flies everywhere, and of course like fifteen kids jump on me to protect me. When they found out I had been cut, it was like their own mothers had been killed in front of them. They were bawling. Literally. People were crying because I had been hurt." She looked flatly at Tyler. "Who *does* that? It was too much, so I finally stormed out the door. No one tried to stop me, because I mean, why would they? I'm *me*, after all."

Jackie sighed and took a sip of the coffee, grimacing again. "This is really terrible coffee."

"It might have been longer than an hour," Tyler admitted. "What time is it?"

Taking out her phone, Jackie's face read annoyance as she swiped away some notifications. "It's quarter to eleven."

"Curses!" As if he had super speed himself, Tyler set to work cleaning up the remaining glass as quickly as possible.

"You, uh," Jackie tried to say as Tyler brushed past her, desperate to make a few rounds before the clock struck. "You need some help?"

Wordlessly, Tyler tossed a broom at her. She caught it with both hands, dropping her coffee in the process and spilling it on the floor. "I got it," he started, but she held him back at a broom's length with a small glare.

"No, stop. I *think* I can handle this. It was my fault anyway."

90

So, the two of them worked, making piles of glass in the corners of the store. With the extra set of hands, Tyler was amazed at how fast they got the task done. He didn't think he'd been moving slowly before, but working beside Jackie provided great motivation for him to be his best.

When the aisle of clocks chimed eleven, Tyler leaned against the wall, wiping a trail of sweat from his forehead. Jackie leaned beside him, surveying the store. With the exception of the missing windows, the place seemed almost presentable. You could barely tell there had been a villain attack the night before.

"Nice job," Tyler said, holding up his hand to high-five Jackie. It was only as he stood there, hand frozen in mid-air, that he realized what he was doing. Before his brain had a chance to reprimand him, he found Jackie returning the gesture, their palms touching for a miraculous fraction of a second.

"That was fun," she said, slightly out of breath. "But, why did we rush to do it?"

"Oh, right," Tyler said, slightly embarrassed. "Well, I promised Mike that I'd visit him in the hospital, and visiting hours start at eleven."

"The hospital?" she said with alarm. "What happened?"

"Well . . ." Tyler said, "Okay, so you didn't hear this from me, but do you know exactly *why* Shard fell from the sky during the chase?"

Jackie paused to think about it. "Something went wrong with his power, so the reports say. He was flying to escape Amazinman from ToughCore© when all of a sudden he started letting out bursts of his power, flying haphazardly, and even cracking his own mask. Then he crashed."

Tyler turned his pressed lips into a smile. "That'd be Mike. He was out on patrol with his parents last night, saw Shard flying, and decided to have a little fun. But as he chased below in his car, an exploding billboard hit him and he crashed into a tree. He broke a few ribs and a leg."

Jackie's mouth hung open in awe. "Wow, that's. . . ." she paused to look out the window, hand unconsciously touching her cheek. In a flash, she turned back around, smiling. "Wow! So he's like a real hero then! Do you think he would mind if I . . . if I visited him too? You know, to thank him?" Tyler raised an eyebrow to her, and she let out a tiny laugh, "No, I guess he wouldn't, would he?"

"You can come," Tyler started, standing up and brushing himself off. "But on one condition."

"What's that?"

Tyler's face was one massive, evil grin. "Call him anything but Mike, like Mitch or Matt or Micah. I just want to see how long it takes him to correct you, if he even bothers to at all."

## _Mondays . . . are Mondays_

For the first time in a long time, Tyler felt good about his life. His grades were good, even if they weren't as stellar as some other people's. He had just lived through a villain attack and had a pretty cool story to tell, even if he did play up some of his heroism a bit more than was necessary. Mike had saved the day, even if they couldn't tell anyone, not because of politics but because of just how much destruction Shard caused when he went on his hiccupping rampage. Tyler's finances were in decent shape, even if he couldn't drive against the rain. Hell, he had even had a full conversation with Jackie, even if no one would believe him.

Tyler smiled at the empty store. Who needed attributes when life was *this* good?

Karma's answer came in the form of crashing doors at the front of the store. Tyler lost his grin as the Devil and his Demons pushed one of the doors almost completely off its hinges. Shawn's skin seemed extra-red today, either due to a nasty sunburn or the rage that was coursing through his veins. His muscles flexed with each step he took, and it wasn't long before his eyes set on Tyler.

"You!" his scream all but breaking the newly installed UltraPlexiglass windows.

"Me?" Tyler questioned, but apparently this wasn't the right thing to say. In a few steps, Shawn had Tyler by the shirt, lifting him onto the counter and a few feet in the air as he fumbled for footing.

"You think you're funny?" Shawn growled, squeezing the shirt a bit more.

"Sometimes, yeah." Again, apparently wrong. Shawn lifted Tyler over the counter with two hands and slammed the clerk down onto the tiled floor. Tyler felt his feet go numb at the impact.

"Nobody thinks you're special." Shawn spat in Tyler's face. "No one cares about you, except in one of those 'Oh, poor Tyler' ways. But they don't really care about you. Not really."

"Okay," Tyler said, because he felt like it deserved a response.

"Argh!" Shawn pushed Tyler back against the counter, pacing a few steps away as he rubbed his hands against his gelled horn hair. "I'm going to kill you," he said, as if just reaching the conclusion. "It's the only thing I can do. That'll bring her back for sure."

"Bring her? . . ." Tyler started to say, before realizing the correlation between opening his mouth and pain.

He shut his mouth.

"Jackie," Quentin said helpfully, mouth full of stolen Twizzlers.

Shawn shoved over an entire display case of dust-scented air fresheners, whirling on his friends. They backed against the wall, leaving plenty of room for Shawn to pounce on Tyler, should he wish it. Seeing their fear, he spun his back at Tyler.

"It's your fault!" he shouted again, pointing his finger like a gun. "Your fault she left me!"

Tyler shook his head, confusion circling him. "Wait, what? What do you think *I* did?"

In a single step, Shawn was on him, hands gripping Tyler's shoulders in a none-too-friendly manner. "We had plans yesterday. Plans she blew off to go hang with you and your sad sack of a friend. Then later, we got to talking. The talking turned into a fight. The fight turned into a bigger fight, and before you know it, she's walking out the door, slamming it in my face!" He stopped, incredulous. "She walked out on me! On *me*!"

Tyler couldn't help the small smile that grew on his face, even though he knew it was the stupidest thing he could do.

Shawn slammed Tyler against the counter again, his grip tightening. "I will not *lose* her to some attributeless freak, okay? She was the best, the greatest, the . . . the. . . "

"Crème de la crème?" Max suggested.

All eyes turned to him at that, but he simply shrugged.

94

"So, she's yours, no one else's?" Tyler found himself saying out loud for some unknown reason. His mouth just started making words, and there was clearly no one home checking things through a filter first. Regardless, it got Shawn's attention.

"Of course she's mine," he snarled.

"She's what, your property? Not a full-fledged human being, capable of her own independent thought or actions, right? Without you beside her, she'd just drift for all eternity until the heat death of the universe comes to claim us all?"

Tyler's brain had come back just long enough for that nugget, as if saying, "Sorry, I was out to lunch, what did I miss?" before surveying the situation and calmly back peddling out of the room.

After a few seconds to process what Tyler had said, Shawn grinned. It wasn't a friendly, "Hey, how ya doing?" grin, but more of a predatory one meant to showcase the sharpness of his teeth. "I'm going to enjoy this." The Devil reared his arm back and swung a haymaker at Tyler's jaw.

Tyler ducked the blow, as much to his surprise as Shawn's. The clerk felt his hair part at the attack, and confusion briefly overcame the two combatants. Shawn was the first to snap out of it, pulling the still-attached Tyler closer and picking him up at the waist, heaving him upside-down and slamming him towards the ground headfirst. Tyler barely managed to get his hands out in time to take the brunt of the damage meant for his head. A distinct *crack*ing sound echoed throughout the store.

Howling in pain, Tyler tried to get to his feet, but failed. Shawn pulled back his fist for another blow as Tyler's brain tried to reboot fast enough to decide on fight or flight. Over the store's PA system, Mr. Walsh's voice rang out loud and clear.

"Attention! Attention! We have the right to refuse service to anyone! Please vacate the store immediately! The heroes have been called, and are on their way!"

The three demons glanced nervously towards one another at that, but Shawn didn't seem to pay it any heed. "It's a bluff," he said, walking over to where Tyler was scrambling away on the ground. "Like I said, no one cares about you. In this world, the strong get their way, and you're not strong at all. You're just a weak little fly annoying those who truly deserve everything."

Cradling his right arm, Tyler moved himself against the wall and used it for balance to push himself up to a standing position. "Okay, so I'm a fly," he said, slightly out of breath, "and maybe I'm not as powerful or popular as you are. But I'd rather be an average nobody then a selfish, immature, jackass like you."

Shawn stopped and stared at him.

For a brief and shining moment, Tyler thought he had gotten through to him. He imagined a world where Shawn took his words to heart, and left the store without further incident. He'd turn himself in, spend a few months in anger management therapy, and apologize to all those he'd wronged. He'd finish school, go to college, and enlist in the army to do his service to his country. When he returned, he'd get a job, nothing major, just volunteer work at a local politician's office. He'd discover a passion for helping others, and then run for office himself when a seat was open. As he took the oath for President, he'd recount the day when an average nobody had the guts to stand up to him, to open his eyes and show him just how the world saw him, and help him make a change for the better.

Instead, Shawn's eyes, normally black with white irises, turned as red as freshly spewing blood. His muscles seemed to grow ten times in size, ripping parts of his shirt. The tiles underneath his feet cracked and gave way to the immense pressure he was exerting.

He took a step forward.

Seconds seemed to stretch.

He took another.

Tyler felt his back hit the wall.

He took a final step.

Tyler closed his eyes.

## *Tuesdays are normally uneventful*

"I said, the place looks pretty good, all things considered." Hector leaned against the counter, both hands propped up to maintain his balance, his pixie wings fluttering thoughtlessly behind him. "I heard the heroes had to get called in for some disturbance yesterday, too. Real rotten luck you're having there."

"Hmmm?" Tyler said, still not really listening. Hector motioned to Tyler's arm, which rested currently in a sling. The healers had helped fix the bruises to his stomach and ribs, and repaired the arm Shawn had broken, but he still needed time to fully recover on his own. "Oh, yeah. That. It's . . . been an eventful few days."

"I bet. Speaking of events!" Hector reached over and placed a few of the protein bars on the counter. "These things tasted terrible, nothing like any strawberry I've ever tasted. But hey, I like to support local businesses, and I figure another week can't hurt, am I right?" He smiled, but his eyes were searching for something else. "Right?"

Tyler rubbed at his throbbing head with his un-slung hand, massaging his temple. "Listen, Hector, I just don't have time to play this part of your little fantasy life, okay? We both know why you're here, so do you want to buy the damn drink or not?"

"I . . . I mean . . . what . . ." Hector blinked, unsure of how to respond. "Sorry," he added quickly, turning to leave.

Tyler closed his eyes, focusing on his composure.

"Wait, Hector!" he said, running around the counter and catching up with the man before he could leave. With his good arm, he spun the man around as another customer entered. "I'm sorry, I didn't mean to snap at you, I've had a tough few days and it's not right of me to take it out on someone else."

"It's . . . okay. . . ." Hector replied sullenly. His eyes found it difficult to focus on Tyler.

"No, it's not. So, here's the truth. We're actually not going to have any of those drinks in stock anymore. I finally figured out the online system. But I know a place that does sell them." He took a step forward, placing a hand around Hector's shoulders and motioning with his sling. "All you need to do is head out of the parking lot, heading right. Take a right on Main Street, then a right on First Street. When you see Primary Street, take a right. Finally, turn on Prime Street, it should be the first store you come across."

Tyler took a step back from the man and shrugged. "Sorry I couldn't be more help."

Hector stood there, drawing out the instructions in the air, then studied Tyler's face. The clerk hoped that the smile he wore looked as genuine as he felt. After a few seconds, Hector beamed at the clerk.

"Ah, it's alright," he said, patting Tyler on his good shoulder. "Who knows, maybe this is for the best. Sure, it's a bit farther away than I'd like to go, but I'm sure the exercise will do me good. I might even make it part of my new daily routine!" Hector smiled again. "I'll see you around, Tyler. And, uh . . . thanks," he said before walking out the door.

Tyler watched Hector leave, and let the sun from outside warm him as the door closed. Smiling to himself, he turned around and almost crashed into Jackie.

"Ah!" he shouted, falling a step back. "When did you get here?"

"How do you do that?" she asked, voice more solemn than he expected.

"Do . . . what?" he asked carefully. He looked around to make sure he wasn't going to be surprised by anyone else.

Jackie shrugged. "You always know what to say to people."

"I don't"—

"But it's more than that." She took a step closer, forcing his darting eyes to settle on her face. He glanced at her cut, which looked as if it was starting to scar. "You know you're the only person who doesn't see me?"

"What?" he asked, voice rising in pitch. "That's impossible Jackie. I can't *not* see you." And he meant it, at least more than the current literal sense.

In response, she shook her head. "I think it has to do with your attribute."

"My . . . attribute?" he parroted.

"Mmhm." Jackie hesitantly raised her hand to touch at the space just to the side of Tyler's right eye.

"Two different colored eyes isn't an attribute," he said, pulling away though he knew he'd regret it later. "It's called heterochromia. Anything with a name that complicated is due to genetics."

Jackie smirked, drumming her fingers on the counter as she waited for him to continue. When he remained silent, she said, "Um, all attributes are genetic, right?" Jackie pulled back her hand but stayed close to him. "Tyler, you . . . you're different than you think you are. You see people for what they are, like certain jackasses who will not be named." She forced a smile. "I couldn't see that."

"He does have a certain . . ." Tyler started, but he cut himself off.

"What's more," she fumbled for the words to say, "you see me as a regular person. Do you know how long it's been since I've entered a room *without* people spinning around to look at me? It's unsettling."

"Just to be clear," Tyler said, "you *like* the fact that I ignored you?"

"Kinda twisted, huh?" Jackie replied with a snicker. A few seconds passed before she said, "You know . . ." her voice trailed off as she pretended to look at the newest square fans on display, "I have it on good authority that there's a pretty cool Viking movie that just opened up."

Tyler blinked in surprise, happiness spreading across his face like the glow from a morning's sunrise.

*Tuesdays* . . . he thought, unable to stop his grin. *Tuesdays are normally uneventful.*

*Normally.*

*Mark Ballweg has been a member of the Northern Montgomery County Writer's Group for three years.*

*Some writing exercises start with a phrase, some random words, a picture, or a memory prompt. Others work out a dramatic problem. This one is—*

### Sunday Drive

### By Linda Meyer

Sweat pooled at my back as I peeled my legs off the cheap plastic upholstery. In the back seat, my sister was stretched across the seat reading. Maybe calling "Shot gun!" was not all it was cracked up to be.

My eyes felt heavy as the wind whipped my hair around my face while I nodded off to sleep. The thumping of the tires played a rhythmic lullaby.

I woke to a loud whacking sound, like someone was beating on the roof with a stick. My mother was gripping the steering wheel as the car zigzagged back and forth across the 3 lane highway. Her white knuckles clenched the wheel, a small groan escaped her lips, and her eyes were filled with panic. My body ping-ponged back and forth between the door and my mother's seat. I grabbed the dashboard in a desperate attempt to stop the beating while we continued to swerve and the tires squealed.

"What is happening?" I shouted as we picked up speed.

"It's the tire!" My mother yelled as the car left the pavement and began to roll. Time stopped, my body, strapped in for the ride, flipped over and over. In slow motion, Fig Newtons and pop cans slapped against my head as the spin cycle continued. We were spun around like clothes in a dryer that was certainly not set to the gentle cycle. Screams filled my ears. Three voices harmonized with terror.

The sound of glass breaking shocked us into silence. Our car settled upside down with a loud screech. I hung from the seatbelt and sobbed. My mother reached over, unlatched my seat belt, and caused me to fall to into a sea of shattered glass. With pebbles of glass stuck in my hands and knees, I frantically looked for the door handle, clawing, searching for the lever to freedom. Finally, I opened the door, falling into the dry summer grass. Gulping air, I crawled away from the car, feeling the glass shards grind further into my skin. The car was a crunched piece of metal, wheels pointed toward the sky, still spinning in the still air, like a beetle on its back.

My sister was on the ground at the back of the car, the back window, still intact, was on the grass next to her. Hugging her knees, she rocked back and forth. Blood polka dotted her yellow shirt.

Sirens filled the air, cars pulled over, and people gathered around us. Someone covered my shaking shoulders with a towel, my knees knocked together with fear. Blood streaked my arms and legs.

The Paramedics arrived and I watched my mother block them from getting near us. Hands on her hips, her slight figure puffed up to the size of a linebacker, she put her hand out like a police man stopping traffic. The paramedics tried to step around her, but stopped at her insistent head shake.

The sun pelted us with heat, while by standers, whispered in quiet clusters, and time stood still. One woman squatted next to me with her hands on my shoulders. I shook loose from the women and crawled over to my sister. Her eyes were closed and she had a wet cloth on her head. With a shaky hand, I took her hand and squeezed. She opened one eye and tried a smile, but it was more like a grimace. Silently, we sat together, as the ambulance lights flashed, voices buzzed like bees and the blood pounded between my ears.

My mother was circling the car, pointing out to no one, that it was ok to drive. Her third trip around, she finally noticed us. Bending down, she patted my sister's shoulder, and touched my head, before returning to her laps.

"Girls, I think we are almost ready to get back on the road," she announced as my sister and I stared at her.

A policeman squatted down next to us, "Your mother is in shock, meaning she isn't quite understanding that the car is not drivable. Where were you headed?"

"My grandma's," I croaked, my throat was dry; the heat from the road shimmered and rolled into the grass, baking us.

"Does anything hurt?" He asked. My sister and I shook our heads, bending our arms and legs to prove it.

The police officer pulled our belongings out of the wreckage. Fig Newton and pop cans spilled out as he tugged at our suitcases.

My mother stuck her head into the twisted mess, "I need my cigarettes." Her skirt too was sprayed with blood and there was a tear in her blouse. Trails of blood ran down her legs. She ran her fingers through her hair as she leaned on the car, instructing the Policeman on how to find them.

With hands still clenched, my sister and I stiffly walked over to the police car and slid into the back seat.

The Police officer helped my mother into the front seat while she continued to argue with him about getting back on the road, in our car. The air conditioning coated our baking skin with sheen of cool.

Peering out the back window I gaped at the car, smashed up against a bridge, the only thing that kept us from rolling into the water below.

The knight checked the girth around his horse's belly one last time. As he stepped away, he ran a hand over the leather of his high-backed saddle, smoother in places where it had been worn to a shine. Saddlebags bulged at the back, filled with blankets, cookware, and other evidence of his camp from the night before.

His destrier whickered and shifted his weight, turned his great black head and lipped at the knight's white surcoat, which draped over the dented steel plates and chainmail of his armor. The knight cupped a palm over the horse's chin and absently stroked a sleek shoulder with a leather glove.

The smell of charcoal and something less pleasant, less clean, drifted up from the valley to the hilltop, causing the knight's nose to wrinkle. He looked out to where black fingers of burnt earth clawed outward from the valley's depths, slashing through the emerald grasses and weeds. The valley descended from the hilltop where the knight stood in the shape of a crescent; at the far point, the knight could just make out the mottled grey and tan angles of a cliff face. Despite the crisp morning and soft periwinkle sky, a fog crept from the bottom of that cliff, billowing upward and outward as if the land itself was exhaling.

He heard a thump behind him. A gaggle of townspeople gathered around a wooden chest, bound with iron. They avoided looking into the valley, and instead darted glances back and forth between the knight and the chest. Some had dressed up, wearing brightly dyed vests, fur-lined dresses, and conical hats as if they sought to impress the knight.

One of the men, his robes belted with a gold chain, leaned over and pushed back the lid of the chest. "Thank you for answering our call, sir knight," he said. "We promised a reward for your help. Here 'tis."

The knight avoided staring at the chest. He thought it important not to appear greedy for the coin. Instead, he cleared his throat and said in a voice that ranged through the crowd, "Thank you, goodman. Are you the mayor of Argentot?"

The man touched the gold at his waist and bowed. He gestured again at the chest. "Please—look."

The knight stepped closer and this time peered inside. The morning sun caught and refracted off the contents in the colors of a sparkling sunrise.

The chest held no coins.

With a squeal of joints, the knight ran his fingers through the chest's contents. "Are these—jewels? They're so large, and the shape—"

"Not jewels. Scales. From the beast." The mayor stroked his salt-and-pepper beard with one hand, and hooked the thumb of his other hand into his belt chain.

"But they might as well be jewels, the way they glitter and shine. They'll fetch quite a price once people know where they came from."

The knight slid off one of his gloves and inspected the scales more closely. With his thumb, he rubbed at the surface. It felt rougher than it looked … with tiny iridescent facets dotting the outside. He tried to bend it in half, but couldn't.

The mayor leaned over him, and spoke quickly. "If you kill it, and skin it, imagine how rich you'll be! Rich enough to buy Lord Darcell's castle out from under him, that's for certain. You ever dream of becoming a lord, young knight?"

The knight grunted. "How'd you get these?" His fingers lingered in the pile of scales.

"Found 'em. On the ground. Most of them are broken, see? We think it shed them, like the serpent it is."

The knight braced his hands on his bent knee and heaved himself back to his feet, the metal rings of his coif swishing and clashing against the edge of his breastplate. "Did it shed them while it was attacking your village?"

One of the women in the crowd behind them murmured something the knight did not catch and another put an arm around her, pulling her close. He grimaced. He hadn't meant to raise bad memories.

"Well, as to that," the mayor said, looking off into the valley, "the creature has never come as far as the town."

The knight frowned. "Then it's struck at people on the road? Or bothered farmers in the fields?"

"It has eaten several sheep."

"Several sheep," the knight repeated.

"Ah," the mayor said, raising a hand, "but the people of Argentot are frightened, sir knight. It's only a matter of time before it comes to the town. Few, I think, will survive when that day comes."

The knight shook his head. "But if it hasn't hurt anyone—"

The mayor caught him in his light blue gaze. "I didn't say it hasn't hurt anyone, young man. A number of people have tried to vanquish the beast in its lair. One brought back some scales before he ... succumbed." He nudged the chest with a foot. "The rest did not return."

"Hmm..." the knight said. "Well, that does sound like a threat." He tugged at his surcoat to set it straight on his shoulders, and took another look at the open chest.

The mayor cleared his throat. "Are you willing to risk it, sir knight? To protect our town?"

The knight tore his gaze from the glinting scales and pursed his lips. "Yes."

*    *    *

*George paused in the kitchen doorway where his mom was loading the dishwasher. "I'm going over to Dylan's house for a while."*

*The dishes rattled as his mother maneuvered a plate into the rack. She straightened. "Did you remember to clean your room? We've got company coming this weekend."*

*"Yeah, Mom."*

*"I expect you home by ten."*

*"Mom. I'm fifteen. No one has a curfew that early."*

*His mother frowned. "All right, eleven. I know it's Friday, but you have to mow the lawn in the morning."*

*"Okay. Bye." George dodged through the living room and out the front door. Dylan's house was a couple of blocks away, near the local park. Though the September evening was muggy and warm, his feet crunched on the leaves that had already begun to fall. In the near darkness, George heard the scraping of crickets. Something brushed against his cheek, moth wings or mosquito legs, and he walked faster.*

*"We're going to the park," Dylan said, when he opened his front door. The news was playing on the TV and something clattered in the kitchen. Dylan didn't let George inside. Instead, he grabbed a backpack that was next to the door, and shouldered George back out onto the porch. George trailed behind as Dylan trotted down the steps onto the walk.*

*"I thought we were going to play Xbox in the basement," said George.*

*"Plan's changed. Angela and Noah are meeting us."*

*George flushed and was glad of the dark. "Angela?" he asked, trying to be casual.*

*"Yeah," Dylan said, "Angela," in a breathy falsetto. He fluttered his eyelashes, and tucked his hands under his chin, making smooching noises with his lips.*

*"Shut up." George's brain was still playing catch up. "Why the park?"*

*"Well, my parents might be clueless, but we can't exactly get drunk in the basement without one of them wandering down there." He adjusted the strap of the backpack on his shoulder and something inside clinked.*

*"Wait, what's in there?"*

*"I liberated something from the liquor cabinet. Someone gave it to my dad, but he just wants beer. It'll be months before anybody*

111

notices." *Dylan stopped and set the backpack on the ground. Reaching inside, he pulled out a bottle with a long, thin neck. "Check this out."*

*George took the bottle, and turned its label face up. He squinted at the label in the light of the streetlamps down the block. "Gold... Goldschlaah..."*

*"Goldschläger." Dylan grabbed the bottle by the neck and held it up to the street lamp. George leaned his head down a few inches toward the shorter Dylan and looked up through the glass bottle. He spotted dark flecks floating around inside. "It's this cinnamon stuff that has real flakes of gold in it."*

*"No way."*

*"Yeah—and you're supposed to just drink them."*

*"Real gold? Wouldn't you want to—keep them? They've got to be worth something."*

*Dylan shrugged, and stuffed the bottle back into his bag. "It's not a lot of gold. Those flakes are real thin."*

*George remained silent the rest of the way to the park. After a bit, they passed the house of his second-grade teacher—Mrs. Thompson. His mom lit up and gushed whenever they ran into each other around the neighborhood—*see how big Georgie has grown!*—but he wished she didn't live so close.*

*Real gold. It was like treasure in a bottle. Drinking it would be even cooler than that video he'd seen on YouTube of somebody eating a ten-dollar bill.*

*   *   *

The knight grimaced as he trudged back to his horse. Because of his audience on the hill, he chose not to lead his destrier over to a boulder to mount from a higher height. Instead, he heaved himself up from ground level, the weight of his armor dragging at him. He glanced at the crowd, but no one seemed to appreciate his prowess.

As his horse shifted beneath him, he slung the straps of his shield over his left arm and then held out an imperious hand. Flicked his fingers. Waited. One of the townsmen scuttled forward, scooped his lance off the ground, and carefully deposited it in his palm. The weapon might look grand to the villagers, but its painted red stripes flaked and the wooden shaft had warped somewhat. Still, it wasn't for show—the foot-long iron tip was tapered to a wicked point. Even in the dim light of the morning, it flashed slick and silver. He had oiled and sharpened it the night before. Pausing briefly to inspect the shaft of the lance for cracks, the knight propped the end in its leather cup on the side of his saddle.

He passed one last look over the people gathered on the hillside. The women wrung their hands. One fluttered a white handkerchief at him; her red eyes suggested that she needed it more than he did. None of the men met his gaze. The man with the gold belt jerked his head up and down in an officious nod.

"Good luck, sir knight. We'll pray to see you safe and victorious."

Raising an eyebrow, the knight lowered his visor, the *clank* ringing too loudly.

The destrier plodded down the side of the hill into the folds of the valley. Horse and man followed a dried-up stream bed. Gnarled trees, shaggy with moss, lined its banks. Some of the trunks tipped sideways toward the stream, thirsty old men with their branches dipping downward to grab a drink.

Halfway down the valley, the knight and his horse entered a foul-smelling fog. It was hard to know where the edges of it began, but the daylight dimmed even as the sun rose higher. The smell of burnt charcoal lay heavier here. The pair had crossed several blighted areas already, the horse snorting at the charred vegetation under its hooves. A bitter scent of decay clung to the back of the knight's throat.

As they edged past the bend of the valley and turned toward its far end, the trees shrank and shriveled into blackened stumps. The last branches fell away and the knight could see the broken trees running toward the opening of a cave mouth gouged out of the cliffside. He reined in and stood in his stirrups. His heart pounded. In the pillowing embrace of the fog, the cave's entrance loomed dark and hazy, its depth unknowable. A huge mound of broken rock and clods of dirt, punctuated by rust-red clay, partially blocked the right side of its mouth.

The horse tossed his head and tried to prance, but his big plate-sized hooves smacked against the rocky ground, and the jolts made the knight grit his teeth and mutter.

A drop of sweat slid down the knight's face inside his helmet, barely missing his eye before slipping down to pause, quivering, above one nostril. He wrinkled his nose to try to dislodge it, while his hands clenched around lance and reins. His horse jiggered sideways, and the knight swore as the unexpected movement nearly unseated him.

Ahead, he surveyed the dark cave. Currents of fog roiled outward in unhurried waves from its opening. The knight grimaced. Just like his destrier, he didn't want to go in there.

"Come out, vermin!" he hollered. "The good people of Argentot have asked me to rid this valley of your loathsome presence!"

Though fog gobbled up the sound, the knight imagined gray shapes swirling in the mist. He squinted through his visor, hunting for movement more substantial than curls of water vapor and smoke.

After a minute, he kicked his horse forward and rode into an avenue of black stumps, but these were not trees. A large heap sprawled almost at his feet with four dirty white stumps protruding from its belly—leg bones of another destrier. Its saddle lay several paces away, flipped over. Its tanned leather underside looked out of place amidst the dull red, white, and black of the rest of the valley. On his left, what the knight had taken for clumps of red clay now revealed themselves as blood smears and hunks of flesh, crawling with black flies. The few incongruous fluffs of white came from a sheep's fleece. Shards of armor poked out of the rocks, and larger pieces lay in twisted piles. The knight spotted at least three other bodies of horses. The graying arches of their ribs reared up out of chests, crusted with dried blood.

A breeze blew through the valley, and carried the fug of rot through the holes in his helmet. He turned his head to one side and fought a battle with his gorge. It was worse than he had expected. He wondered how many other knights the mayor had sent into the valley before him.

Movement ripped the knight's attention from the gore at his feet. His horse whinnied and retreated several steps backward and sideways away from the cave entrance.

An orange-red glow filled the mouth of the cave. The knight squinted as flickers of sunlight caught on a shape emerging from the shadows, a massive flank covered in burnished iridescent scales. A foot crunched into the rocks outside the cave. It flexed claws thicker and longer than the knight's thigh. With steady grace, another foot emerged, then the tip of the snout, before finally the awesome expanse of its chest broke into the light.

As the dragon slid forward, the valley brightened. The knight squinted against the flashing glints of ruby, topaz, and carnelian on the dragon's hide. Despite the persistent smog, the scales were ten times—no, a hundred times—more dazzling than the broken pieces in the townspeople's chest.

The knight took in the length of the creature's jaws and the heft of its fangs. When one burning sapphire eye flicked in his direction, framed by a swirl of smoke from its black nostrils, he had to shut his mouth in order to swallow. He had no illusions about what those ivory teeth would do to his armor should they close around it.

The knight loosed a long, stuttering breath. It was everything he had ever coveted, everything he'd ever feared, wrapped up in one glorious beast.

\*     \*     \*

*Goldschläger tasted like cinnamon and fire, sweet and syrupy and disgusting. George choked on his first swig, and barely managed to keep from spitting it out. He'd gulped too much. It hit his stomach like bang snaps exploding on concrete, and the fumes went up the back of his throat and burned in his nose. He'd had beer before—once again, courtesy of Dylan's smuggling—but it had*

116

been nothing like this. He was glad it was dark and no one could see his face.

Then Angela snickered. "George's turning green!"

Maybe it wasn't as dark as he thought.

Ducking his chin, he passed the bottle to Noah on his left. The four of them huddled on one of the playground's upper levels, the metal bars digging into their backs. A circus-themed roof tented over the platform, while a lone street lamp at the park's entrance cast long shadows through the bars. Bugs rustled in the weeds and little shadows darted against the navy sky.

Noah brushed overlong black bangs out of his face and took several small sips of the Goldschläger. George wondered if he'd drunk any of the gold flakes. He wanted to ask them to drink carefully, not to jiggle the bottle so the flakes wouldn't float to the top and get sucked out the neck. Was there a way he could collect the bottle at the end without looking like a dork? He wished he could see it in the sunlight and get a better sense of how many flakes were in there.

"Man, that stuff is nasty." Noah leaned forward and held the bottle out for Angela. "Dylan, why'd you bring that? It's like cinnamon mouthwash. But worse."

Angela giggled again and twirled some of her blond hair between her fingers as she took the bottle. George wished that he was sitting next to her, but Dylan and Noah had claimed those spots.

"Hey, at least I brought something." Dylan smacked his lips after taking a big sip. "Ah… feel the burn."

Noah groaned, and swiped at his bangs. "Why am I here again?"

The bottle came back to George, and the liquor went down easier, warm and loose. And the next time Angela giggled, he joined her.

117

*   *   *

The dragon waited. Half in, half out of the entrance to the cave, it eyed the knight while a long, bluish-gray tongue tasted the air.

The knight turned his horse in a few tight circles and maneuvered to a clear alley between the stumps and corpses that littered the dragon's doorstep. The creature's head tracked his movements on a sinuous neck taller than the height of his lance. But the great, broad chest, sculpted with ridges of muscle and bone and suspended on bent legs only a yard or two off the ground, offered too clear a target. With luck, one swift strike with his lance and the tip would drive upward into the beast's rotten heart.

His horse worked the bit between its teeth. Foam bubbled at the corner of its mouth and sweat made its shoulders shimmer like polished onyx.

The knight's own sweat ran like an underground river beneath his layers of leather and steel. Tight muscles turned his movements jerky as he brought his lance up, couching it underneath his arm.

"HIE!" he shouted, and dug his heels into the destrier's sides.

The black horse gained speed. The deep thudding of its hooves overtook the beating of the knight's own heart. His focus narrowed to one spot on the dragon's lustrous chest to the right of its breastbone. His breath bellowed and whistled through his visor and the edge of his shield scraped against his armored leg with each lunge of his horse's legs.

Forty feet.

Then twenty.

Ten.

At the last moment, the dragon reared—*twisted*—swiped out with a front paw, and deflected the lance. But not enough. The knight leaned into the lance even as the dragon's claws tangled with his horse's legs.

The iron tip scored the dragon's side.

The horse screamed. Something snapped as its hindquarters flipped sideways. The momentum of the charge tossed the knight out of the saddle, sending him and his horse crashing to the cave floor. They sank into shadow as the dragon's head swung round. A low, harsh hissing sliced into the darkness at the back of the cave.

The last thing the knight heard was the pattering of broken scales falling onto the rocks like pebbles sifting down in the aftermath of an avalanche.

*      *      *

*After half an hour, Angela stopped giggling. The sloshing of the liquor in the bottle had lightened to a teasing swish. The playground platform had floated off the ground and bobbed gently, weighted down only by the heaviness of their limbs. Sour cinnamon sat on George's tongue.*

*Noah took another sip from the bottle, tipping it way up in the air. Abruptly he spat, angling it out between the metal bars. "Nasty," he muttered. "Those gold bits are just wrong."*

*"Oh, no, there goes the gold," George murmured. Maybe he could come back tomorrow and pan through the mulch for the lost flecks—just like the gold prospectors in California that they'd studied in history class. Would he need water for that? He couldn't remember.*

*Noah put the bottle in Angela's hand, but her fingers didn't close around it. "Hey, take it," he said. "Last sip."*

*George peered at her. Her head was slumped over to one shoulder. "I think she's passed out." He blinked hard and tried to shake off the blur.*

*Dylan slid a hand under her cheek and pushed her head back up. "Angela?" He patted her face a few times, then shook her shoulder, hard. "Yep, she's out." His thin fingers drifted down her face, her neck, to her collarbone. "Well, it's your lucky day, Georgie."*

*"What?"*

*"You can do anything you want to her now."*

*George tried to sit up straighter, and had to prop himself up with his palms flat on the pockmarked metal. "Hey. That's—um. We can't—"*

*Dylan snickered. "Hey, we can't, that's—that's wrong," he parroted in a squeaky voice. "No wonder you've never done anything with a girl. You're too scared." His voice was muffled a little as he shifted closer to Angela. George couldn't make out what he was doing. "Noah, help me with these."*

*"Naw, man. I'm gone." Noah swung his legs over to the steps, and pulled himself up, hitching his baggy pants up as he went. He must have misstepped; his shape lurched and dull metal rang. "Shit!" He reached the ground and wavered, half shadow, half reflected florescent glare, out of the park.*

*"Come on, Georgie, you've got to feel this," Dylan said. Angela's form was now lying, crooked, on the platform. Skin showed gray and pale.*

*George wanted to feel it. "I don't think we should—do that. She's not—awake. Isn't that—bad?"*

*"She'll never know. And look—she won't care. She came out here with us, didn't she?" Dylan leaned lower. Someone*

*moaned—Dylan or Angela?—and there was a wet noise. George wanted to see what was happening.*

*Instead he jerked to his knees and swiped a hand down his face. "Dylan, you should stop." He couldn't breathe.*

*"Dude—she's fine." He saw Dylan's head turn toward him. "If you're not gonna join in, then give me some space. I promise I won't do anything bad. But I can't pass this up."*

*George considered leaving, like Noah had. Dylan wouldn't hurt Angela—they'd been friends since the fourth grade. He wouldn't. All of them went to the same church on Sundays. He pushed himself over to the stairs and began to scoot down them on his butt.*

*       *       *

The smell of burning sulfur and overheated metal woke him. Every few seconds, he heard a wet sizzle like bacon frying over the fire.

The knight shifted his shoulders and turned his head. The dragon's neck curved around in a sweeping bend; its forked tongue lathed over the wound in its flank, dog-like. The gouge he'd made with his spear oozed thick maroon. Steam rose after each pass of the great tongue. The knight had trouble looking away from the sight of it—the ugly dark red trickling over the bright orange-gold of the dragon's scales.

The knight's neck hurt, his chest and arms ached, and his cheek, which had struck the inside of his visor when he fell, bled. He jerked and flailed, rocking like a beetle flipped onto its back, until he regained his feet. The grayish white glow of daylight flickered in his left eye, while a greater darkness pushed at him from the right.

He stood braced inside the mouth of the cave. His right arm trembled like a tree branch in a stiff breeze. Gathering himself, he hunched behind his shield and raised his sword.

The dragon's bulk took up one side of the cave. Its forefeet were still planted by the entrance, though one of its rear legs crouched almost close enough for the knight to reach out and strike.

Neither combatant moved. Both watched the other.

A pearly shimmer glinted off the tops of the huge claws, their tips embedded in the loose rock on the floor of the cavern. Curling into the dimness at the back of the cave lay the length of the dragon's tail. The great shadow of its head hovered in the mouth of the cave like a black sun hanging low against a fog-white sky.

The knight was cornered. Caught like a mouse in a fox's den. He'd had no thought of what would happen after he'd charged the dragon. He'd not considered his predicament if the dragon survived.

As his eyes adjusted to the gloom, light sparked off something on the ground. He risked a quick glance down and caught his breath. The floor of the cave was speckled with shed scales, flashing bright, while dull glints further back hinted at the trove the cave contained.

At his feet, the knight's horse thrashed, lifting its head partway off the ground to groan. The twisted lines of its back legs were apparent even in the dimness of the cave.

The knight cursed, long and low.

The dragon's head lifted. Its tongue flicked the air again.

The knight was weeping. He'd not been able to taste the difference at first—between the sour tang of his sweat and the crisp saltiness of tears. The two mingled as they tracked down his cheeks. But he could feel the moisture now, tipping over the edges of his eyelids.

*One brought back some scales before he … succumbed. The rest did not return.* The mayor's voice echoed in his head. Why hadn't he listened? Why hadn't he thought?

Another hiss slipped into the blackness of the cave and reverberated back, encircling the knight. The dragon's tail began tightening and coiling in great loops, dragging across the rocks and causing them to grind and clatter against each other. Its head wove and dipped in the cave's entrance. Its shadowed eyes burned with their own witchlight.

The strike would come soon.

$$*\qquad*\qquad*$$

*There was another moan—definitely Angela this time.*

*George clung to the metal rail. It was cool and clammy like his fingers. "Dylan, you've got to stop. If she can't wake up, she might need help. We should tell someone."*

*Dylan, his face slashed with shadows, snarled at him. "What the hell, man. We can't tell anyone. We're not supposed to be out here—doing this. My folks. They'd crucify me."*

*"But—what about Angela?"*

*"She'll wake up eventually. Her house isn't far."*

*"You just going to—leave her here?" George jerked upright, too quickly. His stomach flipped. He turned his head and a shower of vomit sprayed over the railings and spattered on the mulch. Some of it might have hit his feet, he wasn't sure. His throat blistered and, even after the heaving stopped, he spat repeatedly to clear out his mouth.*

*"Ewwww..."* Dylan had moved away from the side where George had spewed. George turned back to him just in time to see Dylan's hand slide over Angela's bare stomach. He heard a soft zip.

*     *     *

The dragon's lips curled up from its fangs.

The knight gripped his sword so tightly his fingers ached. He panted through his mouth and coughed on the ash.

His destrier thrashed again.

The dragon lunged, ignoring the knight. It latched its jaws around the horse's neck. After one vicious shake, the destrier's scream cut off.

The knight cried out and almost fell backward, but kept enough presence of mind to take advantage of the dragon's distraction and shuffle toward the entrance of the cave. Every sound made his heart stutter, even the sound of the leather soles of his boots sliding over unseen debris. He made it five feet, ten feet, twenty feet, with sword raised.

But the dragon's head swiveled. Its azure stare caught him. He froze. Without warning, the dragon lunged again, its jaws gaping.

"Ahh!" the knight yelled, throwing up his left arm. The *thunk* of the beast's great head against the knight's shield shivered down his arm and into his chest. Wood splintered. He struck out with his sword, but the blade only nicked the dragon's lip before it clattered off its teeth. A clawed foot swept toward the knight, easily pinning him to the cave wall.

124

*Scritch....*

*Pop!*

The tip of one claw punched through the knight's breastplate. A sharp pain bloomed beneath his ribs as the claw split the leather of his gambeson and punctured his belly. The weight of the dragon drove the claw slowly inward. The knight sucked in his stomach as far as he could. Metal creaked as the claw forced its way in another inch.

The knight screamed.

He banged his cracked shield uselessly against the beast's side. The dragon was too close. Metal screeched. He brought his sword up high and wedged the tip into the web between the dragon's digits, levering it back and forth, gouging great scrapes into his own armor.

The dragon roared as the sword sliced into thinner skin. The knight gritted his teeth and used both hands to hammer the blade deeper. The dragon flinched and yanked its foot backward. The claw ripped free from the hole in the knight's armor with such force that it pulled him forward onto his knees.

Hunching over his wound, the knight propped his sword in the gravel and pushed himself to his feet. But a coil of the dragon's tail whipped out of the darkness and crashed against his side. The force tossed him out of the cave. He tumbled until he landed at the bottom of the earthen mound. The knight scrambled to his knees, scuttled forward a few feet to where his sword lay in the dirt, and heaved himself up, already slashing the air to fend off the next blow.

But the dragon had not followed him. With a dull clack of teeth, it curled in on itself, circling just inside the cave. The cut in its foot coated the rocks red and splattered onto the lighter citrine scales of its belly.

The knight wobbled but managed to keep his feet.

Fog and smoke still clouded the sun, but the knight whimpered with the relief of being out of the cave's smothering gloom. He put the mounded pile of earth at his back. Half of his shield had shattered in his fall. The remainder hung crooked off his arm by one leather strap. His stomach burned even as wetness seeped downward into his wool trousers.

The dragon's bulk blocked the entire entrance, crouching sideways with its wounded flank tucked to the inside. Now that they were out in the open again, the weak sunlight lit up the creature's gemstone scales. The knight squinted again at its reflected brilliance, even as his heart gibbered at the fantastic beauty. Without thought, his grip loosened on his sword as his attention wandered from the dragon's weaving fangs toward the perfection of its skin.

A fly buzzed around his helmet. He flinched and brought his attention back to the dragon's face. It could overtake him in a moment. One bound and a snap of its teeth would end him. Yet, it waited.

He should run. Shouldn't he? If he ran away up the valley, perhaps the dragon wouldn't chase him, injured as it was. He flushed scarlet to think of facing the villagers, horseless and defeated.

Or—he could attack the dragon again. Was it worth his life to try for those riches? The beast was wounded already. He'd never have such an opportunity again. His fame and wealth would outshine the sun.

What should he do?

Why wasn't it attacking him? Why was it waiting?

*It has eaten several sheep,* the mayor had said. Sheep. Not people, not oxen, not mules, even though the road ran less than a mile from the dragon's cave.

He gazed into its sapphire eyes and wondered.

\*    \*    \*

*Something fired in the back of George's head. He reached for his phone. "I'm calling my parents." His voice shook.*

*"No—you can't. Stop!" George backed away from him, the two swaying and stumbling over the playground equipment. Dylan grabbed for his arm, missed, and banged his shin on a metal step. He hunched over a railing. "Shit, shit, shit! I can't believe you! We're done—that's it. If you rat us out, everybody's going to know. You'll be finished, asshole."*

*"Dylan—"*

*"No! I mean it. Either you're with me, or you're not."*

*George stood with his phone in his hand. Florescent light from the street lamp glinted off the whites of Dylan's eyes as they stared each other down.*

\*    \*    \*

The dragon twitched. And the knight made his decision.

\*    \*    \*

*The phone connected. "Mom—you've got to come. Something bad's happened. I'm at the park."*

*Emily Wood has been a member of the Northern Montgomery County Writer's Group for three years.*

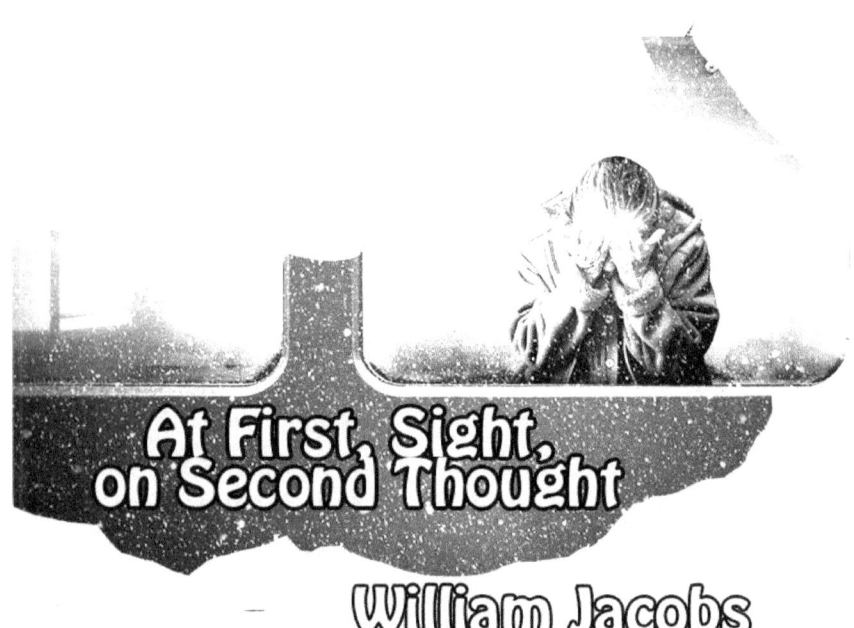

# At First, Sight, on Second Thought

## William Jacobs

Ben looked up from his iPhone just in time to see her. He stared. Something about her drew him. They had so much in common. But why would he think that?

He'd had one of those feelings of being watched— only he wasn't. At least, he didn't think anyone had their eyes on him.

He saw her first.

She was beautiful. Stunning. Even through the hazy Plexiglas, he could make out a classic beauty that a pilot might have painted onto his bomber decades ago. Wavy blonde tresses. Skinny. Eyes you had to fight off an army for. Repeatedly.

*Eyes,* he thought. *If she'd just look up, it would be perfect. Just let me see the eyes with that face.*

The train started pulling away, taking his unearthly vision northward. Her head jerked up from whatever she was reading as if jolted by the train, but rather than backward, her head snapped towards him. Her mouth hung open wide.

The eyes he longed to see met his and a deep pit of black grabbed at him before the jerking motion of the train broke off their connection.

Ben staggered.

When he regained his bearings, the lady on the train was looking about frantically, not finding what she wanted. Ben took a halting step in pursuit of the Metro car, knowing it was futile.

As the train disappeared into the tunnel, she slapped the glass in frustration and shouted something that the smeary, scuffed barrier held captive.

Ben took one step forward as if to run after the train.

*What am I doing?* Ben thought. *Chasing her? What for? A schmuck like me trying to have a shot at a woman like that?*

It wasn't just attraction, though. That could be easily dismissed. He'd seen plenty of drop-dead gorgeous women before and had made nothing of it. Still—

He knew her, but he couldn't remember when he'd seen her before. Weirder, she knew him, too. That was clear enough. She couldn't have been mistaken about who he was; they'd been less than twenty feet apart. If she were that myopic, she wouldn't have noticed his blurry face.

*He knew her. He knew her. He knew her. He knew her. How?*

*Where?*

*Was it important?*

Clearly it was, because he had just crossed the platform in order to board the next train going in the same direction she had. Being late for work meant nothing to him.

A-jitter with what may have been adrenaline or some other cocktail of hormones, Ben desperately, pointlessly, willed the next train to arrive. The overhead display indicated an eight minute wait, which meant an insurmountable head start. It felt impossible. He couldn't meet her unless she was as desperate to meet him as he was to meet her. Unless she got out at the next station to wait for him.

*But why should she be as eager? It was grasping at straws!*

*Then again, why did she seem heart-broken to have missed him? To have been deprived of the chance to talk with him? What did she so urgently need to say to him? What would explain the despair that crossed her face when the train pulled away?*

Mercifully, his racing thoughts were dispersed by a scant ray of hope as the next subway train pulled into the station.

Ben stepped to the platform edge, judging where the doors would end up, foolishly rushing to meet the mysterious woman, even though he could not set forth until the last laggard passenger boarded.

He questioned his judgement yet again.

*What station will she go to? Will she wait for me? Does she know I'll follow? Oh, shit, will she come back to the station I was at? Had she gotten on her train at my station? Or just happened to see me after pulling in to Grosvenor? I don't have her name. I didn't take a photo. I've got nothing!*

*    *    *

"You okay, Ben?"

"Huh?"

"I said, 'You okay?' You looked totally blank in there. Did you hear a word anybody said?"

"Sorry, Clive. I… no, I, uh, I'm kind of out of it. Had the weirdest thing happen this morning."

Ben trailed off, staring at the mug he'd rinsed out in the sink as though it would provide insightful commentary.

"Anything I can help with?" Clive asked, raising the coffeepot along with an eyebrow to offer Ben a cup of the Buttermaker Public Relations break room's finest brew.

"I don't think so." Ben said, sitting down. "It was a girl I saw on the Metro. Yeah, don't look at me that way." Ben turned from Clive's smirk and fingered his coffee cup. "I'm just there and I look up from my phone and there's this goddess sitting in the train going towards Shady Grove. So she sees me looking at her and she gets this look. She kind of leans forward and her mouth opens like she's trying to tell me something. Something important. I mean, it's like she thinks she knows me. Then she starts looking around like she's going to throw the emergency stop handle. Then, she pounds the glass as the train disappears into the tunnel. Thing is, I feel like I knew her from somewhere, too."

"So you knew each other. Why does that have you on Mars?"

"Because I *didn't* know her. It only felt like I did. I recognized her, but didn't know her. Does that make any sense?"

Clive looked at Ben sideways, "No."

"Well, it's got me really out of it. She's all I can think about."

Clive smirked before taking a sip of coffee. He opened his mouth to tease his friend's amorous predicament, but sensing excessive discomfort, decided to play it straight.

"So how do you find her?"

"Should I find her?" Ben hung his head. "I mean, what could happen? She's way out of my league."

"Dude, she wanted to meet you too. It's a done deal."

"But…"

"Fine. Forget about her. Better to leave the fantasies in here." Clive tapped his temple.

Ben stared at the coffee pot, reconsidering his previous refusal of warm beverage. "I did more than look and fawn after her. I followed her on the next northbound train, looking for her at the next station, hoping she'd get out to wait for me."

"Wow, guy," Clive breathed.

"It's not even anything I wanted to do. I had to do it. It's not just because she was pretty. I felt like I knew her… intimately. I can't explain it."

"Obviously!" Clive agreed, taking a seat opposite Ben at one of the polished butcher block break room tables, "Whatever it is, you've got to find her to get your head straight."

"But how? I've got no name, phone number, or anything. I was twenty minutes late to work because of this girl. I'm still… I mean… I didn't even hear every other word in the meeting."

"The subway stations have cameras, you know.  Metro security could tell you which station she got off at."

Ben smirked. "Stalker much? There's no way they'd show me that and they sure as hell shouldn't!"

Clive nodded cordially to a co-worker, who refilled his mug and left, nodding to Clive in return. "What time was it?" Clive continued.

"8? Quarter to 8? Not sure."

"So, what if she's going home the same time of day as you? Maybe a little earlier since she was already on her way and you'd just started. If you're at your home station—Grosvenor, right?—by 3:30, maybe 3, just in case she's a train or two early?"

"That makes sense, but... Again. Stalking."

"Stop making excuses. She *wanted* to see you, remember? All you're doing is making it easy for her. I mean, assuming it went like you said and she was pounding on glass to get out of the car."

Ben moped. "This is stupid. I'm being... I'm obsessing about meeting a girl I have no chance with. What am I, in high school again?"

Ben circled the room.

"She thinks she knows me, but she doesn't. Maybe I'm making the whole thing up!"

Clive flicked the rim of his coffee mug on the table, rotating it. "Then she is, too. The pounding on the glass. Remember? You can't blame yourself for wanting to see where it leads, can you? You seem to be working really hard to talk yourself out of this. Be honest with yourself. Do you want to meet her or not?"

"I'd chop off a finger if I had to."

Clive's eyes went wide. "That's..."

"I know."

Clive looked at the door, then at his coffee cup before slapping his hands on the edge of the table and leaning back in his chair, "Why are you even arguing about it, then? Get to your Metro stop, man, and bring a fucking set of binoculars. You need to find that woman."

Ben raised a finger to object, but Clive quickly interrupted.

"You're ready to lose body parts to make it happen and you've checked out here at work. The best thing you can do for your head and your job is to find out what's up with this woman."

"It's nuts, though. Totally nuts."

"Doesn't matter."

*     *     *

Ben stepped out of the train at the Grosvenor Metro Station as his phone read 2:35. He had at least an hour or more to wait for a woman who may well have sensibly dismissed their meeting as temporary insanity. Clive had been absolutely correct. He was useless at work.

*What should I do?* Ben thought. *Do I search each train as it arrives at Grosvenor? No, I'd end up going three stops to search each one, two cars at a time before the doors closed.*

He rejected the idea. If he boarded any one train, could she be on the train behind it and she'd get off before he searched the one she was on? So much depended on luck. He fumed at himself for missing work for this fool's errand, but he didn't leave the terminal. It had to be done.

Ben was violently thrown out of his reverie by a high-pitched squeal.

His eyes lurched to the platform to his right as a woman closed the distance. Prickles flowed up and down his arms. Once his shock dispersed, he searched through the mane of hair under his chin to find his quarry embracing him.

*It's her!*

Not letting go, the woman gushed, "Oh my God! You came! Oh, thank God!"

Ben sought to free his arms to greet her in return. "Um, hi. Uh. Do we...?"

"I know you!" she exclaimed, hugging tightly, "Where have we met? It must have been ages ago! I've been racking my brain all day!"

Ben put his hands on her shoulders and stammered, "I... I feel like we've met too, but I don't—"

"Have a seat! Let's catch up!" the woman interrupted, tugging at Ben's hand, drawing him into the open shelter housing the station's wooden benches. "Where was it? Where could it have been?"

"Um, college?" Ben offered, sitting next to the elated young lady, finally able to take in the sight of his mysterious...

Ben froze.

So did his new friend.

The pit of black that had sent him reeling that morning returned violently. It blanked out the entire metro station. Nothingness rushed at him. No marking or object distinguished the distance traveled through the void, yet the motion was unmistakable. Ghosts and visions entered into view, before hurtling past. Mountain views, a child on a tricycle. A painting he'd seen in a museum. A leering old man that made his stomach turn. A fetching woman in a bridal gown. A dripping IV bottle and a tube in what he knew was his own arm.

The station returned in a flash of blinding light and he caught himself with the edge of the bench.

He'd been a moment from passing out when he looked to his right and he saw that this new woman had similarly lost her balance.

She brought her fingertips towards her temples, hovering her hands over either side of her head. "Um, are you okay?" she slurred.

Ben's neck muscles felt weak; he looked at the floor, slightly nauseous. "I think so. What was that?"

"I don't know."

They turned towards the tracks in front of them.

"I blacked out," Ben said. "Literally black. The whole place went dark."

"Same here."

The wave of disorientation faded and Ben found his sense of reason again, "I mean I just looked at you and, BAM!"

"Same here. It was when our eyes met. We need to be careful about that."

"No kidding. I could have face-planted on the tile here."

"That rush of black, though? Because of that, I know we've met before."

"At college?" Ben suggested for the second time.

"Didn't go," the lady countered. "High school?"

"Walt Whitman High. You?"

"Ewing."

"Where's that?"

"Trenton, New Jersey. We saw each other there, maybe?" the woman asked.

"Never been to Trenton. Why don't we start with names?"

"Of course!" she said, "I'm Carrie Holmstead! You?"

"Ben Reeves."

Carrie knitted her brow, then shook her head slightly. "It's so strange. I don't remember you, but I know you anyway?"

"Maybe you don't, but I feel the same way," Ben said regretfully.

"Has this ever happened to you before?"

"Pass out after locking eyes with somebody? Never."

"I feel like I've known you my whole life."

"I—" Ben stammered, "I feel like you are my whole life."

"What?"

"After the blackout, I saw stuff I'd done. My entire life passed before my eyes. You know that old expression? It really happened."

Ben looked around for any eavesdroppers, but the enclosure around the benches at this station precluded that possibility. He continued, "But there was extra stuff. I was badly hurt. I was getting married. I saw a mountain. It was this whirlwind of stuff I'd done and other stuff I haven't. I broke off before I could make any sense of it."

Carrie watched as a train pulled in to the opposite platform, "I saw my graduation. A little boy flying paper airplanes. Looking up at our mom in her checkered apron cooking something. And skiing down a bunny slope and being really scared about it."

"Our Mom?" he said with a catch in his throat. "So, memories for you too? Mixed in with other stuff?"

"No, not quite. They were all memories, but not all mine."

"Whose then?"

Carrie looked down at her hands, then to the left and to the right.

Lowering her voice, she asked, "You've heard of past lives, right?"

"Yeah." Ben said dubiously.

"I went to a fortune teller as a kid on the boardwalk in Ocean City. I didn't really believe, but I didn't disbelieve either, you know? It's all junk, I figured. Didn't even cross my mind until just now. Why would it?"

"And this fortune teller…?"

"I'd asked about past lives," Carrie said, "It's one of the things you do when you go to a fortune teller with your friends. She was looking in her crystal ball, like they all do. She told me she saw me as a young man in a subway station looking at a small address book. She said the young man looked up from his address book and looked right at her."

"She saw me?" Ben asked.

"Well, by 'young man', I figured she meant 50 years old or something. She had to be over 80, herself. When I saw you from the train, you looked up at me from your iPhone. I think she saw you through my eyes."

"I had an iPhone, not an address book."

"And what does an iPhone look like twenty years before it's invented?"

Ben stared straight ahead at the tracks.

Carrie resumed, "When she said 'a young man standing by subway tracks,' I figured you were some guy in a bowler hat about to get on 'The Tubes' in New York in the 1930s or something. She was just making up something that sounded good."

"If I'm who she saw, then this isn't a past life. I was alive the same time you went to that fortune teller."

"I think it is, though," Carrie said, weaving her fingers together, "I looked in your eyes and I saw memories. Your memories. I knew your thoughts. I felt what you believe."

Ben's face twisted, "I got that too. Feelings mixed in with the memories, but it all came at me at once. Ideas and history that weren't mine."

"Did our parents divorce when we were younger?"

"What?"

Carrie caught herself, "Sorry. Did *your* parents get divorced when you were younger?"

"Yeah, when I was in fifth grade," Ben answered, uneasily.

"And I remember a bully. He had a minibike?"

Ben's eyes went wide and Carrie turned towards him, but still avoided his eyes.

"It's like a fog," she said, "but I can see what we did."

"So, you used to be me, but now, you're what? Reincarnated?"

"I guess, but it looks like I was brought back overlapping with our—your life." Carrie corrected herself again.

"So I remember nothing of your life because I haven't lived your life yet."

"I guess not, but I remember a lot of what we did. You know, you did."

"This can't be. Can it? We can't be right about this." Ben asked.

Her face colored and her brow furrowed. Ben leaned away from her.

"You know damn well it's true. I know you didn't just ask me that because you doubt it." Carrie's fists pounded the stone Metro bench. "I remember I'm the one who asked it."

Ben paused. He drummed his fingers, caught himself, and stopped the action. He studied her knee, unwilling to chance making eye contact.

"Back on the train. You didn't know why you just *had* to meet a nothing-looking joker like me."

Carrie whirled to Ben and caught his eyes momentarily. She broke off quickly.

"Because I'm not your type at all," Ben finished saying.

"Yes, I know. I was there—here. I remember you feeling that. Then. Now. God, this is weird."

Both were quiet, the moment of eye contact gnawing at them, urging them to connect again.

Neither wanted to give in.

"I saw my memories again," Ben mumbled.

"Me, too. Lots I'd forgotten. Things that happened at least fifty years ago like they were yesterday."

"Maybe some of them were. I saw stuff I did that I'm sure I've never done."

"Maybe you haven't yet," Carrie said. She shuddered. "Let's not do that again."

"Agreed," Ben said, shaking his head vigorously. "What happens to us? I mean, later? My life? Your old life? Our life?"

"I don't think I should be saying anything about that," Carrie said, looking down at her lap. She shook her hands vigorously by her sides, "I can't think straight. When you say things, I'm remembering this conversation and I know what you'll ask and what I'll say. I lose track of who's talking."

"And you can't tell me what Lotto numbers hit tomorrow?"

"You never played the lottery so you were never in the habit of looking at lottery numbers, much less committing any to memory. Even if you had, I'm not that great at remembering stuff now."

"You're remembering this conversation."

"Because. Uhn. This is…"

"Are you okay?"

"I'm remembering this conversation because it was so emotionally intense for us. It's twice as bad now because of the past-present thing I'm doing. I was smarter back when I was you. Maybe you could have handled this. You were into all that 'Star Trek' crap and I…"

Ben smirked, "Now you're wishing you watched more Star Trek so you could have handled this better. The simultaneous double timestream has you screwed up."

Carrie glared at him. "I remember you looking down on me, too. Unh. Any name I call you, I call myself."

She stood up. "We were very arrogant about how smart we were and now that I've—Fuck! You have no idea what it's like to suddenly know in your soul how stupid you are."

"Well, looks like I end up being pretty," Ben consoled her.

"Yeah." Carrie sneered, before sitting down again. "It helped me coast through school, didn't it? I model now. No big shakes, though. I spend time in New York and some in Europe. We get by, but I won't be on magazine covers."

"We?"

"You and me. When you become me later, now." Carrie fought for words, "I can't explain this straight when there's no—"

"We're doing okay, though?" Ben rescued her.

"Yeah, we're doing fine. Could be better, of course. It wouldn't hurt to be rich." Carrie smiled. "I'd thought about what I would tell a past life to do for me: set aside an old comic book or stamp and lock it away in a time capsule for me. But here I am, able to talk to my old self and all you could do is hand it to me."

"Neither one of us gets rich from our time travel, do we?" Ben faux-moped.

"Does this even count as time travel?"

"No. Past lives from the future? Never heard of that before."

"I guess my fortune teller hadn't either."

"So, what do we do from here?" Ben asked, "We've met ourselves, what do we do with this?"

Distantly, a train rumbled in the tunnel.

"I get away from you." Carrie said firmly. "You're going to want to ask me questions about what I've...what we've already done and I'm going to remember any conversation we had while I'm having it and... you don't know what it's doing to my head right now."

"There's nothing that I should try to change?"

"Punch our high school bully in the nose. All bullies are cowards."

Ben smirked. "A little late for that one."

"Yeah, I know. I think the problem is, your memories seem more clear to me since I've lived them twice? Stuff we haven't *both* done yet are foggy. Do you know someone named Tyler?"

"No. Nice name though."

Carrie's neck straightened as her eyebrows lifted, "Oh. Okay...um. Never mind," she trailed off, biting her lip.

"What?"

She looked upward at the smooth, arched glass ceiling that sheltered the subway platform from rain, her shoulders drooping. "This is the stuff you shouldn't know about."

"What?" Ben asked in a panic.

A few would-be passengers' heads swiveled sharply towards them, but Carrie's calm tone of voice soon had them resuming attention to their cell phones. "Tyler. It's a favorite name of yours, isn't it? But you don't know anyone named Tyler?"

"A favorite name? I don't know about that." Ben looked away, blinking unconsciously. "Is it?"

Carrie turned to Ben again, "It's not Tyler Durden, is it? You liked *Fight Club*?"

"Well, yeah, but how did—?"

"It just fit. That's the kind of person we wanted to be. You liked the name. You liked the character. It's what you'd name your son."

"My—" Ben looked down, "Well, now I kind of can't. Can I?"

"You will."

Ben slumped his shoulders, making no attempt to deny what he knew would be true someday. "This whole predestination thing is depressing even if it's about getting to name a kid exactly what I want. Please don't tell me anything else."

"I don't know how many more things I could tell you anyway. Tyler is one of the biggest moments of your life. One of the happiest. So powerful that I could see it through the fog."

Ben looked concerned. "Are you okay?"

"I… I miss him."

"You…"

"I can't remember much about his life," Carrie said, tears threatening to escape her eyes, "But I know how I felt about him. And I want him here."

"Wow."

"This is a bad idea for both of us," Carrie said.

Ben sat frozen, unsure what to do if she started crying. The platform's lights blinked slowly, signaling the arrival of the next train.

Carrie continued, "He… he's gone. I died, or—he died. I left him behind."

She clutched folds of her dress in her hands. "I feel like hugging him, but he's not born yet. It's like he's dead. He's not here with me, but there's nothing wrong. God, he's not even my kid! I'm… I've got to stop thinking about this."

Carrie stood and walked briskly to the train coming to a stop.

Ben followed, unsure if it was the right thing to do.

Carrie heard him behind her and said, "No. Go back. Go home. Live our life. You'll be fine. It comes out okay."

Ben stopped and Carrie bolted inside the subway car.

He let the doors close in front of him, steeling himself to resist the gnawing draw of unsettling, unnatural kinship.

The look in the mirror had to be denied.

William Jacobs is the author of the paranormal *Hell* series: *Sheol* (also titled *The Other Place*), *Litost*, and *Missing Love* (in progress.)

*The story below is a piece of Flash Fiction that was written in fifteen minutes as part of a NMWG Writing prompt. As always, members were provided a couple of elements that we could then incorporate into a narrative. A timer was set and it was off to the keyboard or pencil and pen. Then, in round robin fashion we would share our impromptu creations.*

## Writing Prompt: Ad hoc, library lady, and spaghetti.

### Andrew Hiller

The librarian scowled as the bouncing meatball created an ad hoc bit of abstract expressionism across the floor as it sped towards the rare volumes section. She pursued it, picking up the pace, slipping over the sloshing grease and squish of pureed tomato. Her heart stopped as she crossed the threshold. The smell of aged leather, old paper, and wax had never smelled so garlicy. Worse, the illuminated print had never looked so red, not even when being first copyedited by an overzealous member of the clergy named Theseus Thistledown.

Culprits.

There must be culprits.

*There must be* vengeance she thought, adding to herself that the libraries paltry revenue streams- the twenty-five cents each used books garnered, the fifty-cent copying and printing fees- would never add up. They would delay repairs indefinitely.

She spotted a slender string of yellow. She bent down and picked it up with the dull point of a number four pencil.

Pasta.

Pasta that was shaped like a bow tie.

Her suspicions were sharpening as she imagined who would dare to bring bowties into the library. Perhaps, someone mad that the library's DVD collection had no Andy Griffith Show seasons. No, she was being too literal. Still, the red, the meat, the bow ties, the ad hoc collection of carbs and sugars and foodstuffs… still warm… meant that the evildoer was afoot.

Worse, the evildoer had the same taste as she herself. She stroked the tomato sauce and then a stain on her blouse.

The same. It tasted the same. Someone was trying to frame her. There was only one thing to do. She took a wedge of lemon from her purse and squirted it on her shirt.

She would need to get rid of the evidence. Then, she would be clear to raise the late fee.

Fifty cents a book! She chortled, thunder exploding from an audio book.

**Writing Prompt: Introduce a new form of magic or a superpower that provokes a big societal change and include Hillary Clinton** (Don't worry. The piece isn't particularly political.)

Andrew Hiller

Judy grabbed Tori's wrist. There were too many people here… too many glistening foreheads and smells of bodies. It was overpowering. Still, her little girl, always too adventurous squirmed; the tree legs of people made a perfect maze. Tori didn't care to be a part of history and the lectern was empty. Judy hoped the event would end before snack time, but politicians weren't always that thoughtful. The stage with its dull charcoal floor reflected none of the thirty American flags that drooped in the windless day.

The mic was hot enough to carry the rustle of fabric and the murmur of people. Soon, she would speak. Soon, Hillary Clinton would roar the crowd into a frenzy. The crowd knew the laugh lines of the stump speech, but more importantly hanging from the lights were the sloths.

It seemed strange that they didn't sizzle. The heat generated must have been incredible. If it bothered the extraterrestrial mammals, they didn't react. They just watched with lidded eyes. Judy felt their presence. The weight of their minds heavy against hers. It made her feel sluggish.

Tori tried to dart again. Kids were immune. Kids were too honest. The sloth's telepathic waves flowed around them impotently. For grown-ups though, for nearly one hundred percent of the adult human population, the effect was profound.

Truth. Absolute truth.

Put simply, lies could not be told in the presence of a sloth. It hurt worse than sin even to try. That was why they passed that law. The one that declared that no politician could speak publicly without the presence of at least one sloth. The effect was nearly immediate.

Very few ran anymore. Very few even lobbied. But the biggest change wasn't to politics. It was to reforestation. The need for sloths in business, politics, and elsewhere led to a major effort at reforestation. Habitats were cultivated and carefully watched. Those who would abuse them for profits were quickly ferreted out… or slothed out. The world thus became a greener and more honest place. Judy, still waiting for Hillary Clinton, thought that it had changed everything for the worse.

The virtue of gluttony is the satisfaction of care and comfort. It's the gentle, sated pressure of a full meal eaten, or the insistent whine at about knee-height when your dog doesn't understand why you've stopped scratching its ears. It is the contentment that overrides the learned need for shame, the natural end result of the instincts that drive us to need, the careful weighing of help and harm for the greatest end result. It is the grateful sigh, the irrepressible moan. It's a cheat day, an indulgence, a reminder that too much of a good thing is never truly too much.

*The sin of abstinence is self-denial to the point of pain. It is the gnawing hatred of those that do not, or must not hold back their desires or fulfill their dreams. It is the longing that builds until it is too much to bear, and bursts and swells and destroys anything and everything in its path. It is the pressure of pleasure, or obsession without purpose.*

The virtue of pride is the welling of warmth that belongs at the center of your chest. It is the vital half of the achievements you must hold nearest and dearest, so that their value may do its greatest good. It is a glimmer of self-recognition in the mirror in the morning, and the smile when you see a task done to your satisfaction. It is that which is beautiful and undeniably yours – anything from a child created in your image to a thought made physical in a work of art.

*The sin of humility is walking on eggshells on the path to self-destruction. It is the act of tearing yourself down in the hopes that someone else will raise you back up, and then flaring up in anger when no one takes the bait. It is the act of self-love as poison, or self-hate as a means of attack.*

The virtue of wrath is the will of the man who overturned the moneylenders' tables in the temple of the Lord, and the very same who looked to the leaders of the faithful and called them blind fools and hypocrites. It is the awareness that impels to action, the true calling of the perceptive. It is the force of good against evil, the comic book hero in their cathartic bursts of destruction. It is a power born of love and need, an act of history in a lifetime of complacence.

*The sin of patience is losing sight of the paths impatience can take you down. It is the expectation that hatred and prejudice and violence is a slow and inexorable march towards peace and not a battle that must be won in order for it to end. It is the comfort of willful detachment, and the appeasement that draws weak nations into the clutches of tyrants.*

The virtue of greed is the drive to improve for one and for all. It is the satisfaction of going beyond, the rush of the concept of a hundred and ten percent. It is the moment of stopping and basking in accomplishments and achievements. The tears of an athlete, and the misty notion of cheers and applause and honor and glory and the breathless exertion of victory. It is the urge to bury yourself in the arms of a long-lost lover, and the urge to wind one tongue around another.

*The sin of charity is the promise of impossible things. It is the notion of salvation in exchange for life and limb, and of basic human rights. It is in leaders who are expected to lie in order to attain their leadership, and in con artists lauded for their cleverness and the beauty of their exploitation. It is the illusion of giving, and the shifting of blame when illusions are not enough.*

The virtue of lust is in the moment when a laugh interrupts two people in a tender moment, but only because one of them happened to remember the phrase "diddily doodler" and couldn't help themselves, and in their eagerness they have to share what they've learned with their partner and now they're both laughing, rolling and rolling over each other.

It's the twinge of desire at the back of your brain that distracts you from the task at hand, or anything between the slightest notion of satisfaction and the burst of wanton majesty that comes alongside the fulfillment of the infinite.

*The sin of chastity is condescension. It's wondering why your teenage daughter is pregnant when you had worked so hard to make sure she was never tempted by the sin of sex, and then blaming her for destroying her own life. It's the burden of the victim, compounded by smiling faces on TV screens saying their pain could have been avoided, if only they weren't such a slut. It is a vengeful spirit that craves punishment and a false purity that takes no steps to improve itself.*

The virtue of envy is the drive to improve. It is awareness and control, followed by observation and hypothesis. It is the colloquial notion of dreams, and the breath of air and bursts of adrenaline that power the means to achieve them. It is the necessity that breeds invention, and the invention that breeds freedom from want. It is the means to create something out of nothing, and to introduce that creation to the world. It is passion, ambition, and an eye on the future before the present or past.

*The sin of kindness is in showing permission to your enemies despite clear and present danger, under the guise of the nobility of love. It's in the hearts of the well-meaning people who can look past a pain so intense that it drives the desperate to demand an end to prejudice, to violence, and dare to say "Why can't we just be nice to everyone?" It is the act of allowing hatred to speak to the world and then wondering why innocents are dying. The sin of kindness is about exhaustion and burning yourself out.*

The virtue of sloth is in allowing yourself to rest. It is in sleepy smiles and warm hugs, and the feeling of waking up and knowing that you will not have to leave your bed in the morning, not until you truly want to. It is the tender, maternal shiver that runs down your spine when you see a small, furry creature wrap its long arms around a teddy bear, mimicking its mother or a future tree branch. It is the notion of refreshment, the beauty of a pause, and the urge to stop and stare at a sunset.

*The sin of diligence is in burning your own heart to shreds. It is in the threat of death over a forced evacuation, or a chemical cocktail administered by force to keep you alive at work. It's in little girls lauded in the papers for shouldering the responsibility of medical care their families cannot pay for. It is the glory of working yourself to death, and the expectation to answer emails as soon as they're sent. It's a lifestyle that some call the machine, and others know to be the pinnacle of human achievement. It is destruction without reward, and life taken without truly being lived.*

# *Authors of the NMWG*

**Bryan M. Byrd** (Editor) Coming from an info tech perspective where each character and each decimal position makes a difference, Bryan discovered that the logic of editing fiction and computers are not so different. Every character must be unique and make a difference! Today, when not editing, he's a free-to-roam adventurer whose goal is simply *Surviving Paradise; The Perils and Pleasures of the Caribbean*, expected to debut in 2019; (https://www.goodreads.com/book/show/36560568-surviving-paradise).

**Andrew Hiller** (Editor/Author: A Book of Matches) attempted to travel the road least taken only to fall off, discovering roses, thorns, and *A Halo of Mushrooms*. He has written and hosted for radio, the stage, and is the author of four commentaries selected best of the year by Washington's NPR station WAMU 88.5 FM as well as two fantasy novels: *A Climbing Stock* and the aforementioned *A Halo of Mushrooms*…. More, in a period of geek heaven, he even got an opportunity to write and act with the original Muppets gang.

**Emily Wood** (Editor/Author: Heart of the Beast) moved to Maryland in 2016 after spending seven years in South Carolina.  She compares stalking dragons to keeping up with a pair of seven-year-old twins. Luckily, she has a well-trained steed/puppy to shepherd the fire breathers. Emily is currently finishing up a young adult fantasy novel inspired by the life of Joan of Arc.

 **Mark Ballweg** (Author: A Week in the Life of An Ordinary Teenage Store Clerk) Mark Ballweg is an Information Security professional by day, aspiring author by night. He was born on Long Island and moved to Maryland in early 2014, marrying his wife/long-time editor that year. Currently, he is simultaneously working on a number of low-fantasy novels that he hopes to see published in the future.

 **William Jacobs** (Author: On First Sight, on Second Thought) was born in Milwaukee, Wisconsin and lives near Washington DC. He is the author of two Hellish novels. His first, *The Other Place* - Hell 1.1, was first published July 6th, 2013, followed by *Litost – Hell 2.0 which hit shelves* in April 2016. The third and final installment, *Missing Love* - Hell 3.0, is expected soon... Well, at least before Hell freezes over.

 **Linda Meyer** (Author: The End) is a mother, teacher and a writer. She owns journals full of jotted ideas waiting for birth. When she turned 50, she sat down and wrote what she hoped was the next great American novel. It was not! But, with the help of the Northern Montgomery county writers group, she has found both a home and a group with which to hone her skills as a writer. No, the book is not done, but it is close!

 **Mary Salmonsen** (Author: The Virtue of...) As a real estate author, Mary can honestly say that words form her ideal home. Mary's list of writing projects include graphic novels, poetry, and humorous donut-based fiction.

# If you enjoyed Thursday Stories check out other titles by MCWG authors!

# Andrew Hiller:

*A Halo of Mushrooms is what good fantasy should be
(and almost never is)
Original, colorful, full of wit while managing to comment on life in general.
--Mark Wheatley, Dr. Who*

*It almost strikes you more as a foodie fantasy (eat your heart out, George Martin.) It evolves past that, of course, but Hiller begins his tale with plentiful, savory details. His words are crafted with an unfamiliar cadence that makes even something as mundane
as preparing (and eating) food seem magical and full of whimsy.
--Michael DeAngelo, The Tellest*

# William Jacobs

*William Jacobs has succeeded in sending my mind reeling. Hell 1.0 will force even the most superficial mind to question their morality and take stock of their lives.*
*--Shana Festa*

*This type of ebook is one of the coolest things happening in the publishing industry right now.*

*--Jay Douglass*

www.ingramcontent.com/pod-product-compliance
Lightning Source LLC
Chambersburg PA
CBHW071342170626
46811CB00003B/957